MASTERING SUPPLY CHAIN MANAGEMENT THROUGH LEAN SIX SIGMA

SUBHARUN PAL

BLUEROSE PUBLISHERS

India | U.K.

Copyright © Subharun Pal 2024

All rights reserved by author. No part of this publication may be reproduced, stored in a retrieval system or transmitted in any form or by any means, electronic, mechanical, photocopying, recording or otherwise, without the prior permission of the author. Although every precaution has been taken to verify the accuracy of the information contained herein, the publisher assume no responsibility for any errors or omissions. No liability is assumed for damages that may result from the use of information contained within.

BlueRose Publishers takes no responsibility for any damages, losses, or liabilities that may arise from the use or misuse of the information, products, or services provided in this publication.

For permissions requests or inquiries regarding this publication,
please contact:
BLUEROSE PUBLISHERS
www.BlueRoseONE.com
info@bluerosepublishers.com
+91 8882 898 898
+4407342408967

ISBN: 978-93-5819-850-8

First Edition: February 2024

Contents

Dedication: v

Acknowledgement: vii

Prologue: ix

Preface: xi

Poetic Blurb: xiii

About the Author: xv

Chapter 1: Foundations of SCM and Lean Six Sigma 1

Chapter 2: The Supply Chain Lifecycle: Source to Consumer 3

Chapter 3: Streamlining the Supply Chain: Lean Methodologies 5

Chapter 4: Six Sigma in SCM: Precision and Quality Enhancement 8

Chapter 5: Strategic SCM Design: Harmonizing Development & Delivery 11

Chapter 6: Fortifying Supplier Relationships with Lean Six Sigma 13

Chapter 7: Mastering Inventory: Balancing Supply and Demand 15

Chapter 8: Precision in Demand Forecasting with Lean Six Sigma 17

Chapter 9: Optimizing Transportation and Distribution 19

Chapter 10: Advanced Warehousing: Efficiency and Flow Optimization 21

Chapter 11: Achieving Procurement Excellence: Strategies for Efficient Sourcing 24

Chapter 12: Navigating SCM Risks: Prediction and Mitigation 26

Chapter 13: Quality Assurance in SCM: Standards and Continuous Improvement 28

Chapter 14: Technological Integration in SCM: Leveraging Data and LSS 30

Chapter 15: Leadership and Change Management in SCM 32

Chapter 16: Performance Excellence: SCM Metrics and KPI Analysis 34

Chapter 17: Global SCM Perspectives: Leveraging Lean Six Sigma 36

Chapter 18: Human Capital in SCM: Talent Development and Management 38

Chapter 19: Innovative Approaches in SCM Design 40

Chapter 20: Sustainability in SCM: Ethical and Environmental Perspectives 42

Chapter 21: Practical Insights: Case Studies in LSS-Driven SCM 44

Chapter 22: SCM's Future: Embracing Digital Trends and LSS Adaptation 46

Chapter 23: Conclusion: The Path to Supply Chain Excellence with LSS 48

Appendix A: Essential SCM and LSS Terminology 50

Appendix B: Comprehensive Models in Supply Chain Management 51

Appendix C: Core Lean Six Sigma Tools and Techniques 52

Appendix D: Compliance and Standards in SCM 53

Appendix E: Best Practices and Pitfalls in SCM LSS Implementation 54

Appendix F: Sample Templates for SCM and Lean Six Sigma 55

Appendix G: Global Best Practices in SCM 56

Appendix H: Amalgamation of Disruptive Technologies, SCM, and LSS 57

Appendix I: Integrating Disruptive Technologies with SCM and Lean Six Sigma 58

Dedication:

This book, "Mastering Supply Chain Management through Lean Six Sigma," is dedicated to the relentless and innovative spirits across the globe who strive to redefine the boundaries of efficiency and excellence. To the professionals, students, and enthusiasts in every corner of the world, who see the potential for transformation in every process and the possibility of perfection in every step, this work is for you.

May this book serve as a beacon, guiding you through the complexities of supply chain management and illuminating the path towards mastery with the principles of Lean Six Sigma. Whether you're in a bustling city's corporate office, a remote digital workspace, or a classroom aspiring for change, let this book be a companion in your journey towards creating a more efficient, sustainable, and effective world.

Your dedication, curiosity, and commitment to continual improvement inspire this endeavor. Together, we build a world where excellence is not just an aspiration, but a reality forged through knowledge, innovation, and collaboration. Thank you for being the change-makers, the visionaries, and the unsung heroes in the vast landscape of supply chain management. This book is not just a testament to what has been achieved, but a roadmap to what we can accomplish together.

Acknowledgement:

As I reflect on the odyssey of writing 'Mastering Supply Chain Management through Lean Six Sigma,' my heart swells with gratitude for the constellation of souls who made this dream a vivid reality.

To the passionate mavens in Lean Six Sigma and supply chain management, your unwavering dedication and pursuit of excellence are the beacons that illuminated my path. Your stories, struggles, and triumphs have been the lifeblood of this book.

To my editorial team, you are the unsung heroes who transformed my scattered thoughts into a symphony of words. Your commitment to excellence breathed life into these pages, making every word resonate with those who seek knowledge.

My academic advisors and mentors, you are the sculptors of my thoughts. Your incisive feedback and rigorous critiques have not just shaped this book, but have also profoundly transformed my understanding and approach. I am eternally grateful for your wisdom and guidance.

To my colleagues and peers, our discussions and debates have been a crucible for my ideas. Your intellectual companionship has been a treasure trove of insights, shaping my perspective and enriching this work in immeasurable ways.

To my beloved parents, Mr. Malin Ch. Pal and Ms. Bina Pal, you planted the seeds of discipline and perseverance in my heart. Your teachings have been my guiding light, your ethos of hard work and integrity, the foundation on which I stand.

To my life's cornerstone, Sharmistha, your love and unwavering support have been my sanctuary. You have been the quiet strength behind this tumultuous journey. And to our little bundle of joy, Ayansh, your innocent smiles and laughter have been a reminder of the purest joys of life, teaching me that amidst complexities, simplicity holds profound wisdom.

This book is not just a culmination of my efforts but a mosaic of all your contributions, support, and love. I share the joy and fulfillment of this accomplishment with each of you. From the bottom of my heart, thank you for being the guiding stars on this remarkable journey.

Subharun Pal

Prologue:

"In a world constantly in motion, the art and science of supply chain management stand as pillars of progress and efficiency. The journey towards mastering this intricate field is much like navigating a complex network of interconnected pathways, each decision rippling through the global tapestry of commerce and industry. This book, 'Mastering Supply Chain Management through Lean Six Sigma,' is a voyage into the heart of this dynamic discipline, exploring the transformative power of Lean Six Sigma methodologies in reshaping supply chains.

As we delve into these pages, we embark on a journey that transcends geographical boundaries and cultural differences. We will uncover the universal principles of Lean Six Sigma that have revolutionized supply chain management across the globe, fostering innovation, efficiency, and resilience. From the bustling factory floors to the digitalized warehouses, from local businesses to multinational corporations, the principles laid out in this book are a testament to the unifying power of shared knowledge and the relentless pursuit of excellence.

This prologue serves as your compass, guiding you through the layers of Lean Six Sigma, unveiling its potential to not only streamline operations but also to craft a narrative of sustainable and ethical business practices. As we navigate through these chapters, we invite you to challenge the status quo, to rethink conventional approaches, and to embrace the potential for transformation that lies within the realms of supply chain management."

Preface:

"Welcome to 'Mastering Supply Chain Management through Lean Six Sigma,' a culmination of professional experience and the collective expertise of leaders in the field. This book is more than a guide; it's a bridge connecting the deep-seated theory of Lean Six Sigma with its dynamic application in the realm of supply chain management. It stands as a beacon for professionals, students, and enthusiasts, illuminating a path towards practical understanding and implementation.

In these pages, you'll find an exploration that goes beyond mere methodologies. Here, Lean Six Sigma is presented as a transformative mindset, a key to revolutionizing supply chain management. By incorporating a range of insights and methodologies, this book is designed to elevate your expertise, whether you're a seasoned professional or newly acquainted with this domain.

We traverse through a landscape rich with diverse industry insights and regional perspectives, showcasing the adaptability and universal relevance of Lean Six Sigma principles. This journey is about more than just acquiring knowledge; it's about inspiring change, fostering sustainable growth, and leading with vision in the complex world of global supply chains.

As you delve into this book, I hope it becomes a valuable ally in your quest for mastery in supply chain management. May it empower you to enact significant transformations, drive forward with sustainable strategies, and navigate the ever-changing currents of global supply chains with confidence and expertise."

Poetic Blurb:

"In a world of constant flux and unending change,
Lies a realm where efficiency and precision arrange.
'Mastering Supply Chain Management,' a guide so clear,
Through Lean Six Sigma's lens, we navigate without fear.

In these pages, wisdom and strategy entwine,
Revealing paths where processes and perfection align.
With every chapter, a new insight takes flight,
Illuminating supply chains in a new, transformative light.

From the intricate dance of logistics and flow,
To the subtle art of meeting demand just so,
This book unravels mysteries, layer by layer,
In a world where data and detail are the ultimate player.

Lean Six Sigma, more than a method, a mindset,
In its principles, solutions and success are met.
For professionals, students, and curious minds alike,
These pages hold keys to efficiency hikes.

So embark on this journey, rich and profound,
Where mastery in supply chain management is found.
In the dance of supply and demand, find your part,
'Mastering Supply Chain Management' is where you start."

About the Author:

Subharun Pal, stands at the intersection of academia and innovation, distinguished by his profound knowledge and methodical approach. His academic journey is marked by his involvement with the Swiss School of Management (SSM) in Switzerland and the European International University (EIU) in France, where he delves into a diverse array of disciplines. Pal's expertise spans computer science engineering, disruptive technologies, operations management, logistics, supply chain management, financial analytics, commercial law, and educational theory.

His academic pursuits are further enriched through collaborations with renowned institutions such as IIT Jammu, IIT Patna, IIM Calcutta, IIM Ranchi, Edith Cowan University Perth, CII-Institute of Logistics Chennai, National University of Juridical Sciences Kolkata, Karnataka State Open University Mysore, and Visvesvaraya Technological University Belgaum. Pal's distinguished career is highlighted by recognitions and partnerships with global organizations including The World Bank, KPMG, Cisco, Microsoft, Oracle, and many others.

An embodiment of intellectual excellence, Pal's relentless quest for knowledge is evident in his extensive body of work, which includes insightful research papers, scholarly articles, and innovative patents that hold both international and national significance. His contributions to academic literature, combined with his active role in editorial duties and academic conferences, underscore his unwavering dedication to the advancement of various scholarly fields. This dedication has not only established him as a prominent figure in the international academic community but has also earned him numerous accolades, affirming his leading position in the global arena of intellectuals."

Chapter 1: Foundations of SCM and Lean Six Sigma

Supply Chain Management: An Overview

Supply Chain Management (SCM) is an integral component of modern business operations. It orchestrates the flow of goods and services from the raw material stage through to the end consumer. Far from being a mere logistical function, SCM embodies a complex network of strategies, processes, and relationships. Its goal is to synchronize demand and supply, ensuring products are delivered to the right place at the right time, both efficiently and cost-effectively.

The modern business landscape is characterized by its interdependence, where disruptions in one segment can cascade through the entire supply chain, causing delays, escalated costs, and customer dissatisfaction. This intricate and interconnected nature necessitates robust strategies and tools to enhance operations, reduce waste, and create value for businesses and consumers alike.

Lean Six Sigma: The Confluence of Two Powerful Methodologies

Central to optimizing these supply chain operations is Lean Six Sigma, a methodology that fuses Lean principles and Six Sigma techniques. This combination focuses on process improvement, waste reduction, and minimizing variation.

- Lean: Rooted in the Toyota Production System, Lean methodology is all about eliminating waste in processes. It distinguishes between value-adding and non-value-adding activities, aiming to minimize or eradicate the latter. The seven types of waste (or 'mudas') in Lean include overproduction, waiting, unnecessary transportation, inappropriate processing, excess inventory, excessive motion, and defects.

- Six Sigma: Developed by Motorola, Six Sigma is a data-driven approach that strives to minimize defects and variability in processes. It emphasizes achieving high quality standards by minimizing errors and ensuring consistent, predictable outcomes. A Six Sigma process, for example, targets having only 3.4 defects per million opportunities.

Merging Supply Chain Management with Lean Six Sigma

Integrating SCM with Lean Six Sigma principles creates a powerful framework to optimize the entire supply chain. This synergy aims at identifying inefficiencies, pinpointing root causes of problems, and making informed, data-driven decisions. It allows for the optimization of all aspects of the supply chain, from procurement and production to distribution and customer service.

The benefits of merging SCM with Lean Six Sigma are manifold. They include reduced lead times, lower inventory levels, improved service quality, and enhanced operational efficiency. More importantly, this integration fosters a culture of continuous improvement, where every participant in the supply chain becomes a vital contributor to value creation.

In today's competitive global markets and with increasingly discerning consumers, mastering the integration of SCM and Lean Six Sigma is not just advantageous; it's essential. Such mastery ensures that businesses remain agile, adaptable, and consistently capable of delivering value in a dynamic market environment. The forthcoming chapters will explore these methodologies in greater depth. They will provide valuable insights, strategies, and best practices to effectively leverage the combined strengths of SCM and Lean Six Sigma, setting the stage for unparalleled excellence in supply chain management.

Chapter 2: The Supply Chain Lifecycle: Source to Consumer

Sourcing and Procurement: Foundations of the Supply Chain

The supply chain journey commences with sourcing and procurement, pivotal processes that establish the foundation for production. Sourcing involves a strategic selection of suppliers based on quality, cost, reliability, and their alignment with the company's ethical and sustainability standards. This phase requires a deep understanding of global market trends, supplier capabilities, and risk management. Critical factors such as geopolitical climates, economic stability of supplier regions, and environmental impact assessments are also considered.

Procurement extends beyond the mere acquisition of goods and services. It involves negotiating contracts, managing supplier relationships, and ensuring compliance with legal and ethical standards. Effective procurement strategies are crucial for securing high-quality materials at competitive prices, while also fostering long-term, mutually beneficial relationships with suppliers.

Production and Manufacturing: Converting Inputs into Products

Post-procurement, raw materials enter the production and manufacturing phase. This stage transforms inputs into finished products through a series of operations. Key aspects include process design, capacity planning, quality control, and workflow optimization. The application of Lean Six Sigma principles here aims to streamline processes, eliminate waste, and ensure consistent product quality. Techniques such as Total Quality Management (TQM) and Just-In-Time (JIT) production are also implemented to enhance efficiency and responsiveness.

Warehousing and Inventory Management: The Balancing Game

Effective warehousing and inventory management are crucial for maintaining the balance between supply and demand. Modern warehousing involves sophisticated technologies like Warehouse Management Systems (WMS), automated storage and retrieval systems, and robotics to increase efficiency and accuracy. Inventory management strategies like JIT, EOQ, and ABC analysis are employed to optimize stock levels, reduce holding costs, and improve cash flow.

Distribution and Logistics: The Artery of the Supply Chain

Distribution and logistics are critical in delivering products to the market. This phase involves route planning, fleet management, cross-docking, and efficient load handling. The integration of technologies such as GPS tracking, IoT devices, and Transportation Management Systems (TMS) enhances transparency and control over the distribution process. The increasing trend of last-mile delivery and drone deliveries are also transforming this phase, especially in e-commerce.

Retail and Sales: Meeting Consumer Demands

The retail stage is where products reach consumers. Effective retail management involves inventory turnover analysis, store layout optimization, and consumer behavior analysis. Retailers must navigate the challenges of brick-and-mortar stores and e-commerce platforms, managing aspects such as online customer experience, digital marketing, and omnichannel strategies. The role of data analytics in understanding consumer preferences and tailoring offerings cannot be overstated.

Consumption: Beyond the Point of Sale

Consumption extends beyond the point of sale, offering valuable insights into consumer behavior and product performance. Post-purchase analysis, customer feedback, and product usage data are leveraged to inform future product development and marketing strategies. Understanding the consumer experience is key to building brand loyalty and improving product offerings.

Returns and Reverse Logistics: Completing the Cycle

An efficient returns process and reverse logistics are essential in today's consumer-driven market. This involves managing returns, refurbishing or recycling products, and possibly re-integrating them into the supply chain. Reverse logistics is not only a customer service imperative but also a sustainability practice, reducing waste and environmental impact.

Conclusion: The Dynamic and Interconnected Supply Chain

Mastering the supply chain lifecycle requires an in-depth understanding of each phase and the interconnections between them. The integration of Lean Six Sigma within this lifecycle enhances efficiency, quality, and responsiveness. Businesses must be agile, adapting to changing market demands, technological advancements, and global economic conditions. The supply chain is a dynamic ecosystem, constantly evolving with consumer preferences, technological innovations, and global trends. By comprehensively understanding and effectively managing this lifecycle, businesses can achieve operational excellence, meet customer expectations, and sustain competitive advantage in a complex, global marketplace.

Chapter 3: Streamlining the Supply Chain: Lean Methodologies

Introduction: The Lean Revolution in Supply Chain Management

The infusion of Lean methodologies into supply chain management marks a revolutionary shift towards efficiency and customer-centric operations. Originating from the Toyota Production System, Lean principles focus on eliminating waste and optimizing processes. This chapter explores the transformative impact of Lean on supply chains, detailing its principles, applications, and the profound benefits it brings to supply chain operations.

The Core of Lean: Identifying and Eliminating Waste

Lean methodology is anchored in the identification and elimination of seven types of waste:

- Overproduction: Producing more than demand requires, leading to excess inventory and increased storage costs.
- Waiting: Time lost due to inefficient workflow or delays, leading to reduced productivity.
- Transportation: Unnecessary movement of products or materials, which adds cost without value.
- Inappropriate Processing: Using complex or inappropriate processes or tools that are more than what is required for the task.
- Unnecessary Inventory: Excessive stocks of raw materials, work-in-progress, or finished goods that tie up capital and increase holding costs.
- Excess Motion: Unnecessary movements by employees or machinery, leading to inefficiencies and potential safety hazards.
- Defects: Errors in production that result in rework or scrap, wasting materials and labor.
- Understanding and targeting these waste areas is crucial for implementing Lean methodologies effectively in the supply chain.

Implementing Lean Methodologies in the Supply Chain

Adopting Lean in the supply chain involves several key strategies:

- Value Stream Mapping (VSM): This technique visualizes the entire supply chain process, identifying inefficiencies and opportunities for improvement. VSM is instrumental in pinpointing areas where waste can be reduced.
- Just-In-Time (JIT): JIT aligns production schedules with customer demand, reducing inventory levels and minimizing overproduction.
- Takt Time: Aligning production processes with customer demand to ensure a balanced and continuous workflow, thereby avoiding overproduction.

- Kanban: A visual scheduling system that controls inventory and production. Kanban signals help regulate the flow of materials, ensuring that items are supplied as and when needed.
- Pull System: Contrasting with traditional push systems, a pull system ensures that production is driven by real customer demand, significantly reducing overproduction and inventory levels.
- Continuous Improvement (Kaizen): Kaizen promotes a culture where employees are continuously looking for ways to improve operations, thereby enhancing efficiency and productivity.
- Supplier Integration and Collaboration: Creating partnerships with suppliers to ensure they are also aligned with Lean principles, thereby optimizing the entire supply chain network.

Advanced Lean Tools and Techniques

In addition to these principles, advanced Lean tools and techniques are also applied:

- 5S Methodology: A workplace organization method that helps create and maintain an orderly, disciplined, and productive environment.
- Six Sigma: Integrating Six Sigma with Lean for a more data-driven approach to process improvement, focusing on reducing variation and defects.
- Lean Six Sigma: Combining Lean's focus on waste reduction with Six Sigma's emphasis on quality improvement for a comprehensive approach to supply chain optimization.

Benefits of Implementing Lean in the Supply Chain

The implementation of Lean methodologies brings about numerous benefits:

- Cost Efficiency: Significant reduction in waste leads to lower costs throughout the supply chain.
- Improved Delivery Performance: Streamlined processes result in quicker turnaround times and more reliable delivery schedules.
- Quality Enhancement: Focus on quality control and continuous improvement leads to higher product quality and fewer defects.
- Increased Flexibility and Responsiveness: Lean supply chains can adapt more swiftly to changing market demands and customer needs.
- Enhanced Customer Satisfaction: Timely delivery of quality products improves customer satisfaction and loyalty.

Challenges and Strategies for Effective Lean Implementation

Implementing Lean in the supply chain is not without its challenges:

- Cultural Shift: Adopting Lean requires a fundamental shift in company culture towards valuing efficiency and continuous improvement.
- Employee Engagement and Training: Successful implementation depends on thorough training and active engagement of employees at all levels.
- Integration Across the Supply Chain: Lean principles must be applied across the entire supply chain, requiring coordination and collaboration with suppliers and partners.

- Continuous Evaluation and Improvement: Lean is an ongoing process that requires regular assessment and adjustments to maintain effectiveness.

Conclusion: Lean as a Catalyst for Supply Chain Excellence

Lean methodologies have become indispensable in the quest for supply chain excellence. By embracing Lean principles, organizations can significantly enhance their operational efficiency, responsiveness to customer needs, and overall competitiveness in the market. Lean is not just a set of tools; it is a mindset that requires commitment, collaboration, and continuous improvement to achieve and sustain optimal performance in the dynamic landscape of supply chain management.

Chapter 4: Six Sigma in SCM: Precision and Quality Enhancement

Introduction: Integrating Six Sigma into Supply Chain Management

Six Sigma, a robust, data-driven methodology pioneered by Motorola in the 1980s, has become a cornerstone in modern supply chain management (SCM). Focused on minimizing defects, reducing process variability, and enhancing overall quality, Six Sigma, when applied to SCM, brings transformative improvements, ensuring precision and unmatched quality at every stage of the supply chain.

Understanding Six Sigma in SCM

The primary goal of Six Sigma is to reduce process variations and achieve near-perfect quality. By striving for a target of fewer than 3.4 defects per million opportunities (DPMO), Six Sigma methodology ensures an unprecedented level of consistency, efficiency, and customer satisfaction in supply chain operations.

Implementing Six Sigma in Supply Chain Processes

The Six Sigma approach in SCM is structured around the DMAIC (Define, Measure, Analyze, Improve, Control) methodology:

- Define: This initial step involves clearly identifying and defining the inefficiencies or problems within the supply chain.
- Measure: Quantitative data is collected to measure the current performance of supply chain processes, establishing a baseline for improvement.
- Analyze: Detailed analysis is conducted to pinpoint the root causes of variations or defects within supply chain operations.
- Improve: Solutions and best practices are developed and implemented to resolve the identified issues.
- Control: Ongoing monitoring and control measures are instituted to ensure that the improvements are sustained over time.

Six Sigma Tools and Techniques in SCM

Beyond the DMAIC framework, Six Sigma employs various advanced tools and techniques in SCM:

- Root Cause Analysis: This technique delves deeply into issues to identify underlying causes of problems, providing lasting solutions.
- Statistical Process Control (SPC): SPC uses statistical methods to monitor and control processes, ensuring optimal operation and quality.
- Voice of the Customer (VOC): This approach involves collecting and analyzing customer feedback to understand their needs and refine processes accordingly.

- Supplier Quality Management: Collaborating with suppliers to ensure compliance with Six Sigma quality standards, including training, audits, and feedback mechanisms.
- Process Mapping: Visual representation of each step in a supply chain process helps in identifying inefficiencies, bottlenecks, or points of variation.

Expanding Six Sigma in SCM

In addition to these standard tools, Six Sigma in SCM encompasses broader aspects:

- Lean Six Sigma Integration: Combining Lean methodologies with Six Sigma for a more holistic approach to waste reduction and quality improvement.
- Advanced Data Analytics: Utilizing big data and analytics to drive deeper insights into supply chain processes and performance.
- Change Management: Facilitating organizational change to align with Six Sigma principles, including leadership engagement and employee empowerment.
- Continuous Improvement Culture: Fostering a company-wide culture that embraces continuous improvement, learning, and development in line with Six Sigma principles.

Benefits of Six Sigma in SCM

The integration of Six Sigma in SCM offers extensive benefits:

- Quality Enhancement: Achieving higher consistency and reducing defects leads to superior product quality.
- Cost Efficiency: Streamlined and optimized processes result in significant cost savings.
- Customer Satisfaction: Delivering high-quality, reliable products enhances customer trust and loyalty.
- Risk Management: Predictable, standardized processes reduce operational risks and improve problem-solving capabilities.
- Informed Decision Making: A data-centric approach enables more accurate and strategic decision-making processes.
- Supply Chain Excellence: Enhanced process efficiency, reduced delays, and optimized performance lead to a more agile and effective supply chain.

Challenges in Six Sigma Implementation

Adopting Six Sigma in SCM is not without challenges:

- Complexity in Implementation: Implementing Six Sigma can be complex, requiring dedicated resources and expertise.
- Alignment Across Supply Chain: Ensuring that all supply chain stakeholders, including suppliers and distributors, align with Six Sigma principles can be challenging.
- Continuous Monitoring: Six Sigma requires ongoing monitoring and refinement to ensure its effectiveness.

Conclusion: Pioneering Precision and Quality in SCM

Incorporating Six Sigma into SCM is a strategic approach that fosters precision, quality, and operational excellence. By identifying and eliminating the root causes of variability and defects, and by making data-driven decisions, businesses can build resilient, high-performing supply chains. This not only ensures operational efficiency but also positions companies to exceed customer expectations, paving the way for long-term success in a competitive global market.

Chapter 5: Strategic SCM Design: Harmonizing Development & Delivery

Introduction: Integrating Design with Supply Chain Management

Design for Supply Chain Management (Design for SCM) represents a paradigm shift in product development, emphasizing the integration of design stages with the broader supply chain's capabilities and requirements. This chapter delves into the principles of Design for SCM, exploring how this holistic approach can optimize supply chain efficiency, reduce operational costs, increase agility, and significantly enhance product quality.

The Imperative of Design for SCM

Traditional product design often focuses on the product's functionality and aesthetic appeal. However, this approach can overlook crucial supply chain factors, leading to increased costs, delivery delays, and quality control issues. Design for SCM addresses this gap by ensuring products are designed not just for market appeal but also for efficient manufacturability, streamlined logistics, and environmental sustainability.

Principles of Design for SCM

Design for SCM is underpinned by several key principles:

- Design for Manufacturability (DfM): This principle involves optimizing product designs for easier and more cost-effective manufacturing. DfM includes simplifying product structures, standardizing parts and materials, and designing for assembly efficiency. It aims to reduce manufacturing complexity, minimize production errors, and lower production costs.

- Design for Logistics (DfL): DfL focuses on the logistics aspect, including storage, transportation, and delivery. It involves designing products to be more compact, lightweight, or modular, facilitating easier and more economical shipping and storage. DfL is crucial in reducing logistics costs and enhancing the overall efficiency of the supply chain.

- Design for Sustainability (DfS): This principle prioritizes the use of eco-friendly materials and sustainable manufacturing processes. DfS encompasses considerations like product longevity, energy efficiency, recyclability, and minimal environmental impact. By focusing on sustainability, companies can reduce their ecological footprint and align with increasingly stringent environmental regulations and consumer expectations.

- Design for Adaptability: Given the dynamic nature of markets and supply chains, products need to be designed with flexibility in mind. This involves creating designs that can be easily modified in response to changing market trends or supply chain disruptions.

- Supplier Integration: This involves close collaboration with suppliers during the design phase. Engaging suppliers early on can lead to the selection of more available, cost-effective, and high-quality materials. It also fosters better communication and understanding between the company and its suppliers, leading to more efficient supply chain operations.

Benefits of Adopting Design for SCM

The implementation of Design for SCM offers substantial benefits:

- Cost Reduction: Aligning product design with supply chain processes can significantly cut costs across manufacturing, storage, and transportation.
- Accelerated Market Access: Products designed with supply chain considerations in mind can be manufactured and delivered more quickly, reducing time-to-market.
- Improved Product Quality: Aligning design with manufacturing capabilities often results in fewer defects and higher product quality.
- Environmental Sustainability: A supply chain-centric design often leads to more eco-friendly products, in terms of both materials used and the overall product lifecycle.
- Enhanced Supply Chain Resilience: Products designed with SCM in mind are typically more adaptable to disruptions, ensuring consistent product availability and supply chain stability.

Strategies for Effective Design for SCM

Implementing Design for SCM involves:

- Cross-Functional Teamwork: Promoting collaboration among design, manufacturing, logistics, and procurement teams to integrate SCM considerations from the initial design stages.
- Technological Integration: Utilizing advanced technologies such as CAD, 3D printing, and simulation tools to facilitate efficient design and testing.
- Early Supplier Involvement: Engaging suppliers in the early phases of design to leverage their expertise and ensure material and component feasibility.
- Feedback Loops: Establishing continuous feedback mechanisms throughout the product lifecycle for ongoing design refinement.
- Market Intelligence: Conducting regular market and consumer trend analysis to inform adaptable and relevant product designs.

Challenges in Implementing Design for SCM

While beneficial, Design for SCM faces challenges, including the need to balance innovative design with supply chain practicalities and ensuring cohesive alignment among diverse supply chain stakeholders.

Conclusion: Realizing the Full Potential of SCM through Strategic Design

Design for SCM is more than a design philosophy; it's a strategic approach that ensures products are not only innovative and appealing but also efficiently deliverable through the supply chain. By embracing this integrated approach, companies can enhance operational efficiency, customer satisfaction, and sustainability, effectively bridging the gap between innovation and practical implementation in SCM.

Chapter 6: Fortifying Supplier Relationships with Lean Six Sigma

Introduction: Synergizing SRM and Lean Six Sigma

In the intricate ecosystem of Supply Chain Management (SCM), Supplier Relationship Management (SRM) emerges as a cornerstone for operational success. When harmonized with Lean Six Sigma (LSS) methodologies, SRM transcends conventional limits, fostering not only cost efficiencies but also operational excellence, improved quality, and robust supplier collaborations. This chapter delves into how the integration of LSS principles with SRM can revolutionize supplier interactions, transforming them into strategic, value-creating partnerships.

The Strategic Imperative of SRM in Modern SCM

In the globalized, interconnected commercial world, the significance of suppliers extends well beyond traditional transactional roles. They are integral to the supply chain, profoundly impacting service levels, product quality, and cost structures. Effective SRM goes beyond basic engagement, focusing on nurturing relationships, aligning goals, and maximizing collaborative synergies for collective success.

Lean Six Sigma's Role in Elevating SRM

LSS, with its emphasis on process optimization and quality enhancement, offers a suite of tools and principles vital for advancing SRM:

- Voice of the Supplier (VOS): Analogous to Six Sigma's Voice of the Customer, VOS centers on actively engaging with suppliers to understand their challenges, integrating their feedback, and adapting processes for mutual support.

- Value Stream Mapping (VSM): This technique visualizes end-to-end processes involving suppliers to pinpoint inefficiencies, waste, or bottlenecks. It fosters a culture of joint problem-solving and process refinement.

- Process Standardization: Leveraging LSS to standardize interactions and documentation can streamline communication, reduce errors, and minimize rework.

- Kaizen – Continuous Improvement: This principle encourages ongoing, collaborative improvement initiatives with suppliers, focusing on shared learning and growth.

- Performance Metrics and Analytics: Employing Six Sigma's analytical rigor to develop, monitor, and review supplier-related KPIs ensures that suppliers are consistently aligned with organizational objectives.

Comprehensive Benefits of Integrating LSS with SRM

The amalgamation of LSS principles within SRM offers comprehensive advantages:

- Quality Advancements: A mutual commitment to stringent quality standards and performance metrics ensures suppliers consistently meet organizational quality expectations.
- Enhanced Operational Efficiency: Implementing lean processes leads to reduced lead times, swifter responses, and expedited issue resolution.
- Cost Optimization: Identifying and eliminating inefficiencies in supplier processes yields significant cost reductions.
- Robust Supplier Partnerships: A structured SRM approach, reinforced by LSS, cultivates deeper trust, transparency, and respect between organizations and suppliers.
- Innovation and Collaborative Growth: Joint problem-solving and a unified approach to challenges pave the way for innovative solutions and new opportunities for growth.

Strategies for Effective LSS Integration in SRM

Successful integration of LSS into SRM necessitates:

- Comprehensive Training and Development: Equipping internal teams and suppliers with the knowledge and tools of LSS is essential for a unified approach.
- Cross-Functional Team Integration: Promoting cooperation among procurement, quality, logistics, and supplier teams to ensure comprehensive process improvements.
- Early Supplier Engagement in Strategic Planning: Involving suppliers from the outset in product development or operational changes facilitates efficiency and innovation.
- Data-Driven Reviews and Adaptation: Continuous monitoring of supplier performance, guided by data analytics, to make informed adjustments and improvements.
- Technological Integration for Enhanced Communication: Utilizing advanced technologies for effective communication, data sharing, and process tracking in supplier relationships.

Navigating Challenges in LSS and SRM Integration

While integrating LSS with SRM offers significant benefits, it also presents challenges such as aligning diverse supplier capabilities with LSS standards, consistent application across all suppliers, and balancing efficiency with innovation.

Conclusion: Crafting Transformative Supplier Partnerships through LSS and SRM

Integrating Lean Six Sigma with Supplier Relationship Management signifies a strategic shift in SCM. By focusing on shared objectives, continuous improvement, and leveraging performance data, organizations can elevate supplier interactions from basic transactions to strategic alliances. This integrative approach is vital in today's multifaceted supply chains, where the interdependence of suppliers and companies is key to achieving sustainable competitive advantage and operational resilience.

Chapter 7: Mastering Inventory: Balancing Supply and Demand

Introduction: The Complexity of Inventory Management in SCM

In the multifaceted world of Supply Chain Management (SCM), effective inventory management is both a critical challenge and a strategic opportunity. While inventory ensures the availability of products to meet customer demands, it also represents a significant investment of capital and resources, incurring storage and handling costs. Mastering inventory management involves a sophisticated balance between maintaining sufficient stock to satisfy demand without succumbing to the pitfalls of overstocking. This equilibrium is crucial for attaining cost efficiency, ensuring customer satisfaction, and enhancing the agility of the entire supply chain.

The Multidimensional Role of Inventory in SCM

Inventory serves several key functions in the supply chain:

- Raw Materials: These are essential stocks maintained to guarantee uninterrupted production cycles.
- Work-in-Process (WIP): These are goods currently undergoing the manufacturing process but not yet completed.
- Finished Goods: These are fully manufactured products ready for distribution and sale.

Each type of inventory plays a unique role and requires distinct management strategies to optimize the overall supply chain performance.

Navigating Challenges in Inventory Management

Several key challenges confront effective inventory management:

- Demand Forecasting Complexity: Accurately predicting customer demand is crucial but often complicated by market volatility and consumer behavior changes.
- Lead Time Variability: Uncertainties in supply lead times can disrupt production schedules and sales strategies.
- Seasonal Demand Fluctuations: Many products experience seasonal demand, requiring careful inventory planning to avoid shortages or excess stock.
- Product Lifecycle Changes: The introduction of new products or the phasing out of older ones can create unpredictable demand patterns.
- Economic and Market Influences: External factors like economic downturns, currency fluctuations, or geopolitical events can significantly impact both supply and demand.

Strategies for Optimizing Inventory Management

Effective inventory management strategies include:

- Advanced Demand Forecasting: Utilizing sophisticated analytical tools and methodologies to predict future demand more accurately.
- Strategic Safety Stock Levels: Calculating and maintaining optimal safety stock levels to mitigate supply chain risks without excessive inventory buildup.
- Economic Order Quantity (EOQ) Analysis: Determining the ideal order quantity that minimizes the sum of ordering and holding costs.
- Just-In-Time (JIT) Principles: Implementing JIT to align production and procurement closely with real-time demand, thus minimizing unnecessary inventory.
- Systematic Cycle Counting: Conducting regular and systematic inventory audits to maintain accuracy and inform decision-making.
- Vendor Managed Inventory (VMI) Integration: Collaborating with suppliers to manage inventory levels effectively, enhancing efficiency, and reducing administrative burdens.

Leveraging Technology for Inventory Excellence

Advancements in technology are critical in modern inventory management:

- Predictive Analytics and Machine Learning: Applying advanced data analytics and machine learning algorithms for more precise demand forecasting and inventory optimization.
- IoT and Real-Time Tracking: Implementing IoT solutions for real-time inventory tracking and management, enhancing visibility and control.
- Cloud-Based Inventory Systems: Utilizing cloud-based solutions for scalable, integrated, and accessible inventory management across the supply chain.

Conclusion: Achieving Strategic Advantage through Inventory Management

Effective inventory management is not merely about maintaining stock levels; it's about strategic alignment with demand, leveraging technological advancements, and adopting Lean Six Sigma methodologies to optimize the supply chain. These practices not only ensure operational efficiency and financial prudence but also establish businesses as responsive and reliable entities in a competitive and ever-evolving market landscape. Through mastering inventory management, companies can transform their inventory from a static asset into a dynamic, value-adding component of their supply chain.

Chapter 8: Precision in Demand Forecasting with Lean Six Sigma

Introduction: Refining Demand Forecasting in Supply Chain Management

Demand forecasting is a critical function in Supply Chain Management (SCM), pivotal for aligning operational activities with future market demands. Its accuracy significantly impacts inventory management, production planning, and overall customer satisfaction. Integrating Lean Six Sigma (LSS) methodologies into demand forecasting processes enhances precision, minimizes errors, and improves overall efficiency, proving essential for modern, dynamic SCM.

Strategic Importance of Accurate Demand Forecasting

Effective demand forecasting underpins the strategic planning and operational execution within SCM. It guides decisions regarding the production scale, inventory levels, and logistics planning. Inaccurate forecasts can lead to severe implications such as excessive inventory, stockouts, wasted resources, and missed market opportunities. The sophistication of forecasting methods directly correlates with the ability to navigate market complexities and maintain competitive advantage.

Incorporating Lean Six Sigma in Demand Forecasting Processes

LSS offers a comprehensive toolkit for refining demand forecasting:

- Voice of the Customer (VOC): This key Six Sigma tool involves in-depth analysis of customer data and feedback to accurately gauge market demands and trends.
- Process Mapping in Forecasting: Mapping the demand forecasting process identifies critical stages, potential inefficiencies, or sources of error, providing a blueprint for systematic improvement.
- Root Cause Analysis for Forecasting Errors: A methodical approach to identifying underlying causes of inaccuracies in forecasts to implement corrective measures.
- Statistical Process Control (SPC): Utilization of statistical techniques to monitor and control the forecasting process, ensuring consistency and reliability.
- Design of Experiments (DOE) in Forecasting Models: Experimenting with different variables and models in a controlled setting to identify the most effective forecasting techniques.
- Kaizen for Continuous Forecasting Improvement: Implementing an ongoing cycle of improvement, ensuring forecasting processes adapt to changing market conditions and data insights.

Advanced Strategies in LSS-Enhanced Demand Forecasting

Building upon fundamental LSS principles, advanced strategies in demand forecasting include:

- Predictive Analytics and Big Data: Harnessing vast datasets and predictive analytics tools to extract deeper insights and refine forecasting accuracy.
- Machine Learning and AI: Implementing AI and machine learning algorithms to analyze complex patterns and improve forecasts continuously.
- Integrated Cross-Functional Collaboration: Encouraging collaborative forecasting efforts involving sales, marketing, finance, and supply chain departments to capture a holistic market view.
- Real-Time Data Integration: Incorporating real-time market and environmental data into forecasts for dynamic and adaptive planning.

Multifaceted Benefits of Precision Demand Forecasting

Integrating LSS into demand forecasting delivers multiple benefits:

- Enhanced Forecast Accuracy: Reducing variability and errors in forecasts leads to more precise demand predictions.
- Optimized Inventory Management: Accurate forecasts result in better inventory control, reducing instances of overstocking and stockouts.
- Operational Agility and Efficiency: Accurate demand predictions enable quicker responses to market changes and efficient resource allocation.
- Improved Customer Satisfaction: Ensuring product availability aligns with market demand enhances customer service and satisfaction levels.
- Cost Reduction and Profit Maximization: Enhanced forecasting accuracy can significantly lower costs related to excess inventory and lost sales opportunities.

Conclusion: Elevating SCM through Advanced Demand Forecasting

Employing Lean Six Sigma methodologies in demand forecasting represents a strategic enhancement in SCM. It ensures a high level of accuracy, responsiveness, and efficiency in meeting market demands. By leveraging customer insights, continuous improvement practices, and advanced analytical techniques, businesses can optimize their supply chain operations, align with evolving market conditions, and maintain a strong competitive stance in the ever-changing global marketplace.

Chapter 9: Optimizing Transportation and Distribution

Introduction: Elevating the Role of Transportation and Distribution

Transportation and distribution are the lifeblood of effective supply chain management (SCM). Far more than merely moving products from one location to another, these functions encompass the art of delivering products timely, cost-effectively, and reliably. In today's global and competitive market, optimizing transportation and distribution is indispensable for operational excellence and customer satisfaction.

The Strategic Imperative of Transportation and Distribution

This segment of SCM involves a complex network of activities, from choosing the right mix of transportation modes (trucks, ships, aircraft) to designing efficient route plans, managing logistics partners, and executing effective distribution strategies. It's a critical process that ensures a seamless journey of goods from production facilities to distributors, retailers, and ultimately, end-users.

Navigating the Challenges in Transportation and Distribution

Several challenges are inherent in managing transportation and distribution effectively:

- Global Geographical Spread: The extensive distances in global supply chains add layers of complexity, demanding robust planning and execution.
- Volatility of Fuel Prices: Fluctuations in fuel costs can significantly impact transportation expenses, requiring agile financial strategies.
- Regulatory Compliance Hurdles: Adhering to diverse regional and international transportation regulations demands meticulous compliance strategies.
- Variable Demand Patterns: Handling seasonal demand surges or unforeseen market shifts strains existing transportation and distribution frameworks.
- Infrastructure Limitations: Overcoming challenges posed by inadequate or outdated transport infrastructure requires innovative logistical solutions.

Strategic Approaches to Enhancing Transportation and Distribution

To optimize these functions, several advanced strategies are essential:

- Technology Integration: Implementing sophisticated systems like Transportation Management Systems (TMS) and leveraging IoT for real-time tracking and visibility.
- Advanced Route Optimization: Using data analytics and AI to develop the most efficient and cost-effective transit routes.
- Employing Multi-modal Transportation: Adopting a blend of transport modes to navigate bottlenecks or inefficiencies effectively.

- Optimizing Warehouse and Distribution Center Locations: Strategic placement of these facilities can dramatically reduce transit times and costs.
- Building Strong Logistics Partnerships: Forging reliable alliances with carriers and third-party logistics (3PL) providers to enhance service quality and efficiency.
- Sustainability Initiatives: Integrating eco-friendly practices and technologies in transport operations to minimize environmental impact.

Enhancing Transportation and Distribution with Lean Six Sigma

Incorporating Lean Six Sigma (LSS) methodologies can further refine transportation and distribution:

- Lean Principles for Waste Reduction: Identifying and eliminating non-value-adding activities in logistics processes.
- Six Sigma for Variability Reduction: Applying Six Sigma tools to minimize inconsistencies in logistical operations, ensuring predictability and reliability.
- Continuous Improvement Culture: Embracing a continuous improvement mindset to perpetually enhance transportation and distribution processes.

Benefits of Streamlined Transportation and Distribution

Optimized transportation and distribution confer several key advantages:

- Cost Reduction: Enhanced planning and operational efficiencies lead to substantial savings.
- Accelerated Delivery Times: Streamlined logistics ensure quicker, more reliable delivery, improving customer satisfaction.
- Increased Reliability and Consistency: Improved processes and partnerships result in dependable service quality.
- Environmental Responsibility: Efficient transportation strategies contribute significantly to sustainability goals.

Conclusion: Transportation and Distribution as Catalysts for SCM Excellence

In the dynamic realm of modern SCM, optimizing transportation and distribution transcends cost-saving; it is pivotal for sustaining business continuity, meeting customer expectations, and adapting to the rapidly evolving global market. Through strategic planning, technological integration, and the application of LSS methodologies, organizations can elevate their transportation and distribution operations, turning them into powerful drivers of competitive advantage and overall supply chain success.

Chapter 10: Advanced Warehousing: Efficiency and Flow Optimization

Introduction: Elevating Warehousing in Supply Chain Management

Warehousing, a pivotal element in Supply Chain Management (SCM), transcends its traditional role of mere storage to become a dynamic hub of activity. An optimized warehouse not only ensures smooth product flow and swift order fulfillment but also maximizes space utilization and resource efficiency. As businesses grapple with changing market dynamics and escalating customer expectations, enhancing warehousing operations through advanced methodologies, particularly Lean Six Sigma (LSS), is crucial for maintaining competitive edge and operational excellence.

The Strategic Function of Warehousing in SCM

Warehousing fulfills several critical functions in the supply chain:

- Buffering Against Variability: Warehouses act as strategic buffers, managing the discrepancies between supply production and consumer demand.
- Facilitating Product Assortment and Handling: They serve as central points for consolidating diverse products, enabling efficient handling and distribution.
- Economies of Scale in Transportation: By allowing bulk storage and transportation, warehouses contribute to economies of scale, reducing overall transportation costs.
- Critical Role in E-Commerce: In the era of e-commerce, warehouses are integral to managing the complexities of online order fulfillment and last-mile delivery.

Challenges in Contemporary Warehousing

Modern warehousing faces numerous challenges that necessitate innovative approaches:

- Managing Space Effectively: Efficient utilization of warehouse space is essential, especially during fluctuations in inventory levels.
- Optimizing Inventory Management: Balancing stock levels to prevent overstocking and stockouts, while facilitating rapid access to products.
- Skilled Labor Management: Ensuring the availability of skilled workers, particularly during peak operational periods.
- Technological Advancements and Integration: Implementing and adapting to sophisticated systems like WMS and automation technologies poses significant challenges.
- Handling a Variety of SKUs: Efficient management of an increasing range of stock-keeping units (SKUs) is crucial for operational efficiency.

Strategies for Warehouse Operational Excellence

Several strategies are pivotal for optimizing warehouse operations:

- Implementing Lean Warehousing: Adopting lean principles to eliminate waste, enhance workflow efficiency, and promote a culture of continuous improvement.
- Utilizing Automated Storage and Retrieval Systems (AS/RS): These technologies improve storage density, accuracy, and speed up retrieval processes.
- Zone Picking Optimization: Strategically organizing warehouses into zones to streamline the picking process and enhance order fulfillment efficiency.
- Cross-Docking to Minimize Storage: Implementing cross-docking to reduce handling costs and transit times by bypassing prolonged storage.
- Leveraging Data Analytics for Insights: Employing analytics to understand demand patterns, optimize inventory levels, and anticipate workforce requirements.
- Incorporating IoT for Real-Time Tracking: Utilizing IoT technology for instant visibility into inventory, warehouse conditions, and equipment status.

Advantages of Optimized Warehousing

An effectively optimized warehouse delivers multiple benefits:

- Enhanced Cost-Efficiency: Streamlined operations and reduced wastage contribute to significant cost savings.
- Accelerated Order Processing: Efficient warehouse processes ensure faster order fulfillment, leading to increased customer satisfaction.
- Scalable Operations: Ability to adapt to varying demand patterns and market conditions.
- Increased Accuracy and Reliability: Minimizing errors in order picking and inventory management enhances operational reliability.
- Safety and Risk Reduction: Well-organized warehousing operations decrease the risk of accidents and product damage.

Integrating Lean Six Sigma in Warehouse Management

The application of LSS in warehousing involves:

- Waste Reduction: Identifying and eliminating inefficiencies within warehousing processes.
- Process Standardization: Utilizing Six Sigma methodologies to create standardized, efficient warehouse operations.
- Data-Driven Management: Employing statistical analysis for informed decision-making in inventory and warehouse operations.

Conclusion: Warehousing as a Driver of SCM Effectiveness

In today's fast-paced and complex business environment, warehousing is not just a storage solution but a critical component of effective SCM. By embracing advanced strategies, incorporating technological innovations, and applying Lean Six Sigma principles, warehouses transform into highly efficient, responsive, and strategic assets. This evolution elevates warehousing from a traditional storage function to a key driver of agility, efficiency, and competitive advantage in the broader supply chain framework.

Chapter 11: Achieving Procurement Excellence: Strategies for Efficient Sourcing

Introduction: Rethinking Procurement in the Context of SCM

In the multifaceted world of Supply Chain Management (SCM), procurement stands as a key determinant of an organization's overall efficiency and market competitiveness. Moving beyond the traditional confines of mere purchasing, procurement excellence encompasses a strategic amalgamation of sourcing, analyzing, and relationship-building. This chapter delves into transforming procurement from a basic operational function into a strategic cornerstone that significantly enhances organizational value.

The Comprehensive Scope of Procurement

Procurement extends its influence across various critical dimensions within an organization:

- Cost Management and Optimization: Efficient procurement strategies directly influence an organization's cost structure, opening avenues for substantial savings.
- Ensuring Quality Standards: The quality of procured inputs invariably dictates the quality of final products and services, highlighting the need for stringent quality checks in procurement processes.
- Fostering Supply Chain Resilience: Building robust supplier relationships is key to ensuring supply continuity, especially in the face of market disruptions.
- Catalyzing Innovation: Collaborative supplier engagements can lead to breakthroughs in product development and process optimizations.

Navigating Challenges in Advanced Procurement Practices

Procurement excellence entails addressing a series of complex challenges:

- Managing Diverse Supplier Networks: Especially in a global setting, orchestrating a network of suppliers requires sophisticated management skills and systems.
- Comprehensive Risk Management: Continual monitoring and mitigation of various risks, from supply disruptions to geopolitical shifts and supplier instabilities, are crucial.
- Contract Negotiation and Management: Developing contracts that encapsulate both specificity and flexibility is a balancing act of strategic importance.
- Technological Advancements: Successfully integrating cutting-edge technologies into procurement processes demands dedicated efforts for adaptation and training.

Strategies for Procurement Excellence

Achieving excellence in procurement involves a multifaceted approach:

- Strategic Sourcing: This involves a deep analysis of spending patterns, market understanding, and leveraging buying power for optimal terms and cost benefits.

- Robust Supplier Relationship Management (SRM): Fostering strong, mutually beneficial relationships with suppliers ensures reliability and spurs joint innovation.
- Embracing Digital Transformation: Implementing digital procurement platforms, AI, and blockchain enhances efficiency, transparency, and decision-making accuracy.
- Risk Management Frameworks: Developing and executing a comprehensive risk management strategy to proactively address potential supply chain disruptions.
- Continual Learning and Development: Focusing on upskilling procurement professionals to keep them abreast of the latest trends, skills, and technological advancements.
- Performance Tracking and KPIs: Establishing and regularly reviewing key performance indicators to ensure procurement activities align with broader organizational objectives.

Benefits of Enhanced Procurement Practices

Procurement excellence yields substantial organizational benefits:

- Cost Savings: Strategic sourcing and effective negotiations lead to significant reductions in procurement expenses.
- Quality Enhancement: Strong supplier partnerships underpin access to higher-quality materials and services.
- Proactive Risk Management: Effective risk strategies enhance supply chain resilience and operational continuity.
- Operational Efficiency: Advanced procurement processes and technologies streamline operations, enhancing speed and precision.
- Driving Innovation: Close collaborations with suppliers often result in innovative solutions that confer a competitive advantage.

Conclusion: The Strategic Dimension of Procurement

In modern business ecosystems, procurement transcends its traditional role, evolving into a strategic function crucial for driving organizational success. It's not solely about efficiency in purchasing but about the broader effectiveness in aligning procurement with corporate goals. Procurement excellence, characterized by strategic sourcing, effective supplier management, and technological integration, is pivotal in achieving cost savings, quality improvements, and innovation. This transformation of procurement into a strategic endeavor is indispensable for organizations aspiring to attain sustainable growth and maintain a competitive edge in today's dynamic market landscapes.

Chapter 12: Navigating SCM Risks: Prediction and Mitigation

Introduction: The Criticality of Risk Management in SCM

In the intricate realm of Supply Chain Management (SCM), risk management is a fundamental aspect that dictates the resilience and efficiency of the entire supply chain. With SCM being inherently complex and intertwined with numerous processes, stakeholders, and global networks, it is naturally predisposed to a multitude of risks. These risks, varying from operational hiccups to global disruptions, can substantially hinder a business's functionality and profitability. Effective SCM Risk Management is thus centered around identifying, assessing, and strategically mitigating these risks to maintain continuity and competitive advantage.

Exploring the Breadth of Risks in SCM

SCM risks are diverse and multifaceted, generally categorized into:

- Operational Risks: Including internal disruptions like machinery breakdowns, human resource variability, and technological failures, which can impede day-to-day operations.
- Geopolitical Risks: Encompassing external factors such as political instability, trade disputes, and regulatory shifts in crucial operational or sourcing regions.
- Environmental Risks: Pertaining to natural disasters such as floods, earthquakes, or severe weather events that disrupt logistics and supply chains.
- Economic Risks: Involve fluctuations in global economic conditions, currency exchange rates, and market dynamics that affect demand and supply chain costs.
- Supplier-Related Risks: Concerning issues with suppliers' financial stability, quality management, and delivery timeliness.

Advanced Strategies for SCM Risk Management

Effective risk management in SCM involves comprehensive and proactive strategies:

- Thorough Risk Assessments: Conducting detailed evaluations of the supply chain to pinpoint potential risks, analyzing their likelihood, and assessing their potential impact.
- Supply Chain Diversification: Implementing a diversified approach to suppliers, logistics routes, and manufacturing locations to mitigate the impact of specific risks.
- Technology Utilization: Employing advanced technologies such as Artificial Intelligence, Internet of Things, and predictive analytics for early detection and response to disruptions.
- Building Collaborative Networks: Developing robust relationships with suppliers, distributors, and logistics partners for enhanced communication and joint problem-solving.

- Adaptive Inventory Strategies: Maintaining strategic buffer stocks and safety inventories as safeguards against supply and demand fluctuations.
- Developing Agile Contingency Plans: Crafting flexible action plans for various risk scenarios to enable quick and effective responses to disruptions.

Benefits of Proactive SCM Risk Management

Adopting a proactive approach to risk management in SCM offers significant benefits:

- Sustained Business Continuity: Minimizing interruptions and maintaining smooth operations even during adverse events.
- Cost Efficiency and Loss Prevention: Anticipating and mitigating risks prevent potential financial losses related to supply chain disruptions.
- Enhanced Brand Reliability: Effective risk management positions a company as a reliable and resilient entity in the eyes of customers and partners.
- Strategic Decision-making: Comprehensive understanding of risks informs smarter, more informed decisions across the supply chain.
- Operational Efficiency: Ongoing risk monitoring and mitigation lead to smoother, more streamlined supply chain operations.

Integrating Lean Six Sigma for Risk Mitigation

Incorporating Lean Six Sigma (LSS) in risk management enhances SCM by:

- Lean Methodologies for Waste Reduction: Identifying and eliminating inefficiencies within the supply chain that may pose risks.
- Six Sigma Techniques for Risk Identification and Reduction: Applying statistical and analytical methods to identify, assess, and minimize supply chain risks.
- Kaizen for Continuous Risk Management Improvement: Employing a continuous improvement approach to refine and adapt risk management practices over time.

Conclusion: Mastering SCM Risks for Organizational Resilience

Navigating risks in SCM is an essential facet of modern business operations. With a comprehensive approach to SCM Risk Management, organizations can effectively anticipate, mitigate, and manage risks, transforming potential vulnerabilities into opportunities for improvement and growth. By embedding a robust risk management framework and utilizing Lean Six Sigma methodologies, businesses can navigate uncertainties with confidence, ensuring sustained resilience and maintaining a competitive edge in a dynamic global marketplace.

Chapter 13: Quality Assurance in SCM: Standards and Continuous Improvement

Introduction: Reframing Quality Assurance as a Strategic SCM Component

Quality Assurance (QA) in Supply Chain Management (SCM) transcends traditional views of merely ensuring product or service standards. It represents a strategic, systematic process integral to an organization's success. QA in SCM is not just about defect detection and compliance; it's about fostering a culture where quality is ingrained in every operation and decision. This chapter explores how QA, through continuous improvement and adherence to high standards, can optimize processes, reduce errors, and ultimately elevate the overall quality of offerings in SCM.

The Pivotal Role of QA in Modern Business Dynamics

QA's importance in the competitive business environment is multifaceted:

- Customer Satisfaction and Loyalty: High-quality products and services are crucial for customer satisfaction, leading to increased loyalty, repeat business, and enhanced brand reputation.
- Cost Management and Reduction: Efficient QA processes help in identifying and rectifying defects early, reducing the costs associated with rework, returns, and recalls.
- Compliance and Regulatory Adherence: Meeting industry-specific standards and regulations is essential, making robust QA processes a necessity.
- Sustaining Competitive Edge: Consistent quality is a key differentiator in the marketplace, providing a significant competitive advantage.
- Building Organizational Credibility: A reputation for quality can strengthen a company's position in the market, attracting new customers and retaining existing ones.

Key Components of Effective QA in SCM

Comprehensive QA involves several crucial elements:

- Development of Quality Standards: Establishing specific, measurable quality criteria for products and processes.
- Thorough Process Documentation: Ensuring every step in production or service delivery is documented for consistency and traceability.
- Focused Training and Development: Providing ongoing training to staff at all levels to uphold and enhance quality standards.
- Conducting Regular Audits and Inspections: Implementing periodic checks to ensure continuous adherence to quality standards.

- Robust Feedback Systems: Establishing mechanisms for collecting and analyzing feedback from various stakeholders to inform quality improvements.

Cultivating Continuous Improvement in QA

QA's effectiveness is anchored in its commitment to continuous improvement:

- Kaizen Philosophy: Emphasizing ongoing, incremental improvements involving every employee, from executives to frontline workers.
- Six Sigma Methodology: Utilizing data-driven techniques to identify and minimize defects, enhancing efficiency and quality.
- Total Quality Management (TQM): Adopting a holistic approach focused on long-term success through customer satisfaction and company-wide participation in quality improvement.
- Implementing Quality Circles: Facilitating small groups of employees to voluntarily address and solve quality-related challenges.

Navigating Challenges in QA Implementation

Effective QA implementation in SCM confronts several challenges:

- Evolving Customer Expectations: Adjusting quality standards to align with shifting market trends and consumer preferences.
- Complexity in Global Supply Chains: Ensuring consistent quality across extensive, multinational supply chains.
- Keeping Pace with Technological Advances: Continuously updating QA processes to align with rapid technological changes.
- Cultural Diversity in Global Operations: Integrating a consistent quality culture across varied global teams and operations.

Conclusion: QA as a Foundation for SCM Excellence

In today's evolving marketplace, QA in SCM is a fundamental pillar of organizational strategy. It extends beyond compliance to embody a culture of excellence, permeating every aspect of the supply chain. By maintaining and elevating quality standards, and fostering a spirit of continuous improvement, businesses can effectively meet customer demands and carve out a sustainable path to success. QA in SCM is pivotal not just for operational efficiency but as a strategic driver of growth, innovation, and competitive advantage in the global business landscape.

Chapter 14: Technological Integration in SCM: Leveraging Data and LSS

Introduction: Revolutionizing SCM Through Advanced Technologies and Data Analytics

In the contemporary landscape of Supply Chain Management (SCM), the integration of cutting-edge technologies and comprehensive data analytics, reinforced by the principles of Lean Six Sigma (LSS), is fundamentally transforming supply chain operations. This chapter explores how the synergistic blend of innovative SCM technologies, data-driven insights, and LSS methodologies can dramatically optimize, enhance, and revolutionize supply chain processes.

Technological Advancements Reshaping SCM

The application of technology in SCM introduces transformative changes:

- Enhanced Real-Time Visibility: Utilization of RFID, IoT, and GPS technologies for tracking provides unprecedented real-time visibility into the movement of goods, offering critical operational data.
- Predictive Analytics and Demand Forecasting: Advanced data analytics tools enable sophisticated demand forecasting by analyzing historical trends, market conditions, and real-time data, leading to more accurate inventory management and production planning.
- Automation and Robotics: The deployment of robotic process automation (RPA), AI, and machine learning in various SCM components streamlines operations, enhances accuracy, and improves speed in areas like warehousing, logistics, and customer service.
- Seamless System Integration: Modern SCM systems integrate disparate functional areas—procurement, manufacturing, distribution, and returns—into a unified, efficient flow, enhancing coordination and reducing delays.

Data: The Core of Modern SCM Strategy

Data plays a pivotal role in SCM, enabling:

- Strategic Insights and Decision Making: Leveraging big data analytics for deep insights into consumer behavior, supply chain performance, and market trends.
- Real-time Performance Monitoring: Using KPIs and dashboard analytics for real-time monitoring and management of supply chain operations.
- Proactive Risk Management: Data analysis is key to identifying potential supply chain risks and developing preemptive mitigation strategies.
- Optimized Supplier Management: Data analytics assists in evaluating supplier performance, ensuring compliance, and fostering effective supplier relationships.

Integrating Lean Six Sigma with Technological and Data Capabilities

The fusion of LSS with technology and data offers a compelling synergy for SCM optimization:

- Empirical Process Improvement: LSS's emphasis on data-driven decision-making is bolstered by advanced analytics, providing precise data for process improvement and waste reduction.
- Enhancing Efficiency through Automation: The application of automation and AI aligns with Lean principles to maximize efficiency and minimize manual intervention.
- Facilitating Continuous Improvement: Continuous feedback mechanisms enabled by technology aid the LSS cycle of ongoing improvement, ensuring SCM processes remain agile and effective.
- Customer-Centric Process Optimization: Integrating LSS with CRM systems ensures that SCM processes are continuously refined to enhance customer value and satisfaction.

Challenges in Technological and LSS Integration

Despite the benefits, integrating advanced technology with LSS in SCM involves complex challenges:

- Implementation and Adaptation Complexity: Merging sophisticated technologies with LSS principles requires specialized expertise and a comprehensive understanding of both domains.
- Managing Organizational Change: Effective change management is crucial to ensure smooth adaptation to new technologies and processes by employees.
- Ensuring Data Security and Compliance: With the increasing reliance on data, maintaining its security and adhering to stringent privacy regulations is critical.

Conclusion: A New Paradigm for SCM Excellence

The convergence of advanced technology, extensive data analytics, and Lean Six Sigma principles represents a new paradigm in SCM. This triad offers a comprehensive framework for businesses to enhance operational efficiency, foster innovation, and maintain agility in a dynamic market. By leveraging this integrated approach, organizations can not only optimize their supply chains but also position themselves as adaptive, customer-focused, and forward-thinking entities in the global business arena. This chapter underscores the significance of this synergy in transforming SCM into a highly efficient, responsive, and data-driven system, pivotal for achieving long-term success and competitive advantage.

Chapter 15: Leadership and Change Management in SCM

Introduction: Navigating the Dynamics of Change in SCM

Effective leadership and efficient change management are pivotal in the fast-evolving domain of Supply Chain Management (SCM). The ability to skillfully guide organizational restructuring, implement new technologies, and steer strategic redirections is crucial for SCM leaders. This chapter delves into how successful change leadership is rooted in a deep understanding of organizational culture, the imperative of adaptability, and the pursuit of comprehensive transformation.

Organizational Culture: The Foundation of Change Acceptance

The significance of organizational culture in facilitating change is profound:

- Accelerating Change Adoption: Alignment of change initiatives with an organization's intrinsic values and beliefs encourages quicker acceptance and integration by employees.
- Minimizing Resistance: Cultures that emphasize adaptability and flexibility typically exhibit lower resistance to change, facilitating smoother transitions.
- Embedding Sustainable Change: Culturally congruent changes are more likely to become ingrained, leading to long-lasting transformations.
- Cultural Reassessment: When proposed changes clash with existing cultural norms, leaders must either consider a broader cultural transformation or develop strategies to navigate and reshape these cultural barriers.

Adaptation and Agility: Core Principles of Change Leadership

Adaptation is central to effective change management in SCM:

- Proactive Change Anticipation: Leaders must stay informed about industry trends, technological advancements, and shifts in market dynamics to anticipate and prepare for necessary changes.
- Cultivating Organizational Flexibility: Developing an organizational culture that values agility, where teams can quickly adapt to new conditions, is indispensable.
- Transparent Communication: Consistent and clear communication about the motives, benefits, and procedures of change is essential to reduce uncertainties and build trust.
- Inclusive Stakeholder Engagement: Involving employees, partners, and other stakeholders in the change process ensures diverse perspectives, fosters a sense of ownership, and enhances the receptiveness to change.

Transformational Leadership: Beyond Incremental Adjustments

Transformation in SCM implies profound and holistic changes:

- Visionary Leadership: Effective transformational change requires leaders with a clear, compelling vision and the ability to inspire and unite the organization around this vision.
- Risk Embracement: Significant changes often involve exploring unknown territories, necessitating leaders who are willing to undertake calculated risks.
- Commitment to Resource Allocation: Transformation initiatives demand dedicated investment in financial, technological, and human resources.
- Emphasis on Continuous Learning: Organizations prioritizing continuous learning and development are better positioned for successful transformations.

Challenges in SCM Change Leadership

Leading change in SCM involves navigating various challenges:

- Overcoming Human Resistance: Addressing the natural resistance to change, often stemming from fear of the unknown or concern about job security.
- Effective Communication Strategies: Ensuring clear and consistent communication to prevent the spread of rumors and misinformation that can derail change efforts.
- Long-term Perspective: Balancing the need for immediate results with the understanding that true transformational change requires time and persistence.

Conclusion: The Art of Change Leadership in SCM

Mastering change leadership in SCM is a multifaceted endeavor that demands strategic foresight, empathetic people management, and steadfast commitment. By focusing on cultural alignment, fostering adaptability, and envisioning transformative changes, leaders can effectively steer their organizations through the complex waters of change. In the modern business era, characterized by rapid evolution and disruption, the ability to lead and manage change is not merely a valuable skill but a critical necessity for maintaining resilience, achieving long-term success, and securing a competitive edge in SCM.

Chapter 16: Performance Excellence: SCM Metrics and KPI Analysis

Introduction: Mastering SCM Through Strategic Metric Management

In the multifaceted domain of Supply Chain Management (SCM), the effective application and analysis of Key Performance Indicators (KPIs) and metrics are essential for operational excellence. This chapter explores the intricate role of KPIs and metrics in SCM, emphasizing their criticality in optimizing processes, guiding strategic decisions, and fostering continuous improvement.

The Strategic Imperative of KPIs in SCM

KPIs serve multiple pivotal roles in SCM:

- Enhanced Visibility and Operational Insight: KPIs offer a clear snapshot of the supply chain's current performance, identifying areas of operational strength and those needing attention.
- Data-Driven Decision-Making: Utilizing accurate, real-time data from KPIs, managers can strategically optimize processes and address inefficiencies.
- Benchmarking and Goal-Setting: Metrics serve as vital benchmarks for setting realistic, measurable, and relevant targets, aligning day-to-day activities with strategic objectives.
- Fostering Accountability: Clearly defined KPIs delineate responsibilities, ensuring that each stakeholder is accountable for specific aspects of supply chain performance.
- Promoting Continuous Improvement: Regular KPI monitoring establishes a foundation for continuous improvement, crucial for the dynamic nature of SCM.

Essential Metrics and KPIs in SCM

Key metrics in SCM, while variable based on specific organizational needs, generally include:

- Inventory Turnover Ratio: Indicates how frequently inventory is sold and replenished, highlighting inventory management efficiency.
- Order Fill Rate: Measures the percentage of customer orders fulfilled without shortages, reflecting the effectiveness in meeting customer demands.
- Lead Time Measurement: The time from order placement to delivery, with shorter lead times often correlating with higher customer satisfaction.
- Accuracy of Order Fulfillment: Tracks the proportion of orders shipped without errors, directly affecting customer satisfaction and return rates.
- Warehouse Utilization Rates: Assesses the optimal use of available storage space.
- Freight Cost Analysis: Evaluates the cost efficiency of transportation per unit.

- Return on Supply Chain Assets (ROA): Determines the profitability of assets utilized within the supply chain.
- Comprehensive Supplier Evaluation: Utilizes scorecards to assess supplier performance on various criteria, including punctuality, quality, and responsiveness.

Navigating Challenges in KPI Implementation and Analysis

Implementing KPIs in SCM presents various challenges:

- Data Integrity and Reliability: Ensuring the accuracy, timeliness, and consistency of data for meaningful KPI analysis is crucial yet challenging.
- Integrating Quantitative and Qualitative Measures: Balancing the focus between quantitative KPIs and qualitative factors like stakeholder relationships or employee well-being is essential.
- Managing KPI Selection and Focus: Too many KPIs can lead to confusion and reduced focus. Prioritizing KPIs aligned with core strategic objectives is key.

Conclusion: Navigating SCM with Precision Through KPIs

In SCM, performance metrics and KPIs act as indispensable tools for navigating the complex landscape of modern supply chains. They provide actionable, data-driven insights into operational performance, guiding improvements and strategic decisions. By judiciously selecting, monitoring, and analyzing these metrics, organizations can enhance operational efficiency, adapt to market changes, and maintain a competitive edge. This chapter highlights the importance of a strategic, balanced approach to KPI management as a fundamental driver of success and sustainability in SCM.

Chapter 17: Global SCM Perspectives: Leveraging Lean Six Sigma

Introduction: Optimizing Global SCM Through Lean Six Sigma

In the era of globalization, Supply Chain Management (SCM) has evolved into a complex, transcontinental undertaking. The expansion of supply chains across borders introduces multifaceted challenges, necessitating the strategic application of Lean Six Sigma (LSS) methodologies. This chapter explores the crucial role of LSS in enhancing efficiency, maintaining quality, and ensuring consistency in the global SCM landscape.

Exploring the Dynamics of Global SCM

Global SCM encompasses various intricate aspects:

- Geopolitical Influences: International supply chains are often susceptible to geopolitical tensions, policy shifts, and trade disputes, necessitating strategic flexibility and adaptability.
- Cultural Variances: Managing SCM across different cultural landscapes requires understanding and navigating diverse business practices, communication styles, and cultural norms.
- Logistical Challenges: International logistics, including transcontinental shipping, customs, and varying transportation infrastructures, introduce additional complexity to SCM.
- Currency Exchange Variability: Fluctuations in currency rates can significantly influence cost management, pricing strategies, and overall profitability.
- Regulatory Heterogeneity: Adhering to a range of country-specific regulations regarding product standards, safety, and environmental compliance is challenging yet essential.
- Strategies for Risk Diversification: Global SCM allows for risk diversification, such as multi-regional sourcing, to mitigate the risk of localized supply disruptions.

LSS as a Strategic Tool in Global SCM

LSS methodologies provide pivotal benefits in addressing global SCM challenges:

- Standardizing Processes Across Borders: LSS aids in creating uniform processes, ensuring consistent quality and performance globally.
- Efficiency through Waste Reduction: Lean principles target redundancies and inefficiencies in global operations, particularly in logistics and supply chain workflows.
- Maintaining Quality Across Markets: Six Sigma's focus on minimizing variability is crucial in ensuring consistent product standards in diverse markets.
- Enhanced Forecasting Techniques: Six Sigma tools assist in advanced forecasting, considering global trends, market volatilities, and geopolitical factors.

- Cultural Sensitivity and Integration: Lean principles emphasize respect and consideration for individuals, which is crucial in managing diverse global teams and operations.
- Robust Global Risk Management: Employing the DMAIC framework facilitates effective risk assessment, strategy development, and implementation of control mechanisms in global supply chains.

Adapting LSS for Global SCM Challenges

Successful implementation of LSS in a global context involves specific adaptations:

- Ongoing Global Awareness: Continuous learning about international market trends, regulatory changes, and economic conditions is crucial for LSS practitioners.
- Customizing LSS Approaches: Adapting LSS tools and methods to meet the specific requirements of different regions or cultural contexts.
- Effective Cross-Cultural Collaboration: Utilizing communication and collaboration tools effectively ensures that LSS teams across various countries can work in unison.

Conclusion: Navigating Global SCM Complexity with LSS

Lean Six Sigma emerges as an essential strategy for managing the complexities inherent in global SCM. By integrating LSS principles into international supply chain operations, organizations can effectively tackle the challenges posed by globalization. This comprehensive approach not only streamlines operations and enhances quality but also positions organizations to capitalize on the opportunities presented by global market dynamics. In doing so, LSS acts as a crucial enabler for organizations seeking to achieve and maintain a competitive edge in the global supply chain arena.

Chapter 18: Human Capital in SCM: Talent Development and Management

Introduction: The Cornerstone of SCM Success - Human Capital

In the dynamic field of Supply Chain Management (SCM), the significance of human capital cannot be overstated. Amidst rapid technological advancements and evolving market dynamics, SCM relies heavily on a workforce that is not only skilled but also adaptable and strategically aligned with the organization's goals. This chapter delves into the nuances of talent management within SCM, emphasizing the need for strategic placement, skill enhancement, and continuous motivation and development of personnel.

Crucial Role of Human Capital in Modern SCM

Human capital serves several vital functions in SCM:

- Innovation Driving Force: A diverse and skilled workforce is instrumental in propelling innovation, introducing new perspectives, and crafting solutions to intricate SCM challenges.
- Boosting Operational Efficiency: Employees adept in modern technologies and methodologies are crucial for streamlining operations, reducing errors, and curtailing delays.
- Strategic Decision-Making Contributions: The workforce plays a central role in strategic decisions, leveraging insights from data analytics, market trends, and customer feedback to refine SCM operations.
- Facilitating Adaptability and Change: The workforce's capability to embrace and adapt to new methodologies and technological changes is key to successfully implementing advancements in SCM.

Advanced Strategies for Talent Management in SCM

Effective talent management in SCM is achieved through a comprehensive strategy:

- Strategic Recruitment and Selection: The process of identifying and recruiting individuals with the required skills and aptitudes sets the foundation for a robust talent base.
- Continuous Training and Development: Providing ongoing education and development opportunities ensures the workforce remains abreast of industry changes, SCM best practices, and technological innovations.
- Performance Management and Goal Alignment: Regular assessments and feedback, coupled with clear goal-setting, align individual efforts with organizational objectives, fostering a culture of accountability and high performance.
- Career Development and Succession Planning: Establishing clear career paths and succession plans is essential for employee motivation, reducing attrition, and securing leadership continuity.
- Employee Engagement and Wellbeing Initiatives: Actively promoting employee engagement and wellbeing enhances productivity and cultivates a positive organizational culture.

Addressing Challenges and Capitalizing on Opportunities

Managing human capital in SCM involves addressing specific challenges and seizing opportunities:

- Skill Gap Analysis and Bridging: Identifying and addressing skill gaps through targeted training initiatives is crucial due to rapid technological and methodological evolutions in SCM.
- Promoting Diversity and Inclusion: Cultivating a workforce that values diversity and inclusivity brings a range of perspectives, enhancing creativity and fostering innovation.
- Retention Strategies for Top Talent: Implementing comprehensive strategies for talent retention, including competitive compensation, growth opportunities, and a supportive work environment, is imperative in a competitive job market.

Conclusion: Synergizing Human Capital with SCM Objectives

Human capital and talent management are pivotal in navigating the complex landscape of SCM. By investing in people – through effective recruitment, ongoing development, and retention strategies – organizations can build a resilient and dynamic supply chain capable of driving innovation, ensuring efficiency, and responding adeptly to change. This synergy between human capital and SCM is foundational, propelling organizations towards operational excellence, adaptability, and sustained growth in an ever-evolving business environment.

Chapter 19: Innovative Approaches in SCM Design

Introduction: Revolutionizing SCM with Forward-Thinking Designs

In today's global market, Supply Chain Management (SCM) extends beyond traditional logistical functions, evolving into a strategic element crucial for competitive success. This evolution, driven by globalization, rapid technological advances, and shifting consumer expectations, necessitates innovative SCM designs that are agile, resilient, and customer-centric. This chapter delves into the progressive models and frameworks reshaping SCM, highlighting their role in providing businesses with a strategic advantage.

Emergent Models and Frameworks in Contemporary SCM

Innovative SCM design involves rethinking traditional models to adapt to modern challenges:

- Digital Twin Integration: Implementing digital replicas of physical supply chains allows for advanced scenario simulation, improving decision-making, and risk assessment.
- Adoption of Circular Supply Chain Models: Transitioning to circular models focuses on sustainability, emphasizing resource reuse, waste reduction, and recycling, aligning with the circular economy principles.
- Decentralized Supply Chain Strategies: Diversifying resources across multiple locations, this approach mitigates risks and enhances adaptability to market changes and disruptions.

Resilience and Agility: Essential Attributes in Modern SCM

The importance of resilience and agility in SCM has been underscored by recent global events:

- Resilience as a Key SCM Feature: The ability of a supply chain to withstand disruptions and maintain operational continuity is paramount.
- Agility in Responding to Market Dynamics: The capability to rapidly adjust and reconfigure supply chains in response to fluctuating market demands or supply issues.
- Innovative SCM for Resilience and Agility: Incorporating elements of resilience and agility into SCM designs ensures businesses can meet customer needs consistently, even in uncertain and volatile environments.

Harnessing Lean Six Sigma for SCM Innovation

Lean Six Sigma (LSS) serves as a pivotal framework in fostering SCM innovation:

- Process Optimization through LSS: Utilizing LSS methodologies to identify inefficiencies and streamline processes, paving the way for innovative SCM solutions.
- Incorporating the Voice of the Customer (VOC): Aligning SCM designs with customer needs and expectations, as emphasized in Six Sigma.

- Data-Driven Innovation: LSS's analytical approach supports informed decision-making, ensuring that SCM innovations are both creative and practical.
- Cultivating a Continuous Improvement Mindset: Embracing LSS's principle of ongoing refinement, ensuring SCM designs remain cutting-edge and efficient.

Navigating the Challenges in Innovative SCM Design

Implementing innovative SCM designs involves addressing specific challenges:

- Commitment to Continuous Learning: Staying abreast of evolving global trends, technologies, and regulatory landscapes is essential for innovative SCM design.
- Localizing and Customizing SCM Innovations: Adapting innovative approaches to specific regional or business-specific contexts for effective implementation.
- Fostering Collaborative Innovation: Promoting cross-functional and external partnerships enhances the scope and impact of SCM innovations.

Conclusion: Innovation as the Bedrock of SCM Strategy

Innovation in SCM design is no longer a luxury but a strategic imperative. Adapting to the rapidly changing business landscape requires SCM models that are not only efficient and resilient but also attuned to global trends and consumer demands. Through embracing innovative frameworks and leveraging methodologies like Lean Six Sigma, organizations can effectively navigate the complexities of global supply chains, achieving sustainable growth and maintaining a competitive edge in the market. This chapter underscores the need for continuous innovation in SCM as a fundamental driver of success in the global business arena.

Chapter 20: Sustainability in SCM: Ethical and Environmental Perspectives

Introduction: Elevating Sustainability in SCM

In an era where global awareness and responsibility take precedence, Supply Chain Management (SCM) has expanded its focus to encompass sustainability. This shift in perspective emphasizes not just efficiency and cost-effectiveness but also the integration of ethical practices and environmental stewardship. This chapter provides an in-depth exploration of how Lean Six Sigma (LSS) facilitates this sustainable transition, fostering practices that align with ecological conservation and ethical integrity while maintaining economic viability.

Foundational Pillars of Sustainable SCM

Sustainable SCM is anchored on three fundamental pillars:

- Environmental Stewardship: Central to sustainable SCM, this involves minimizing the environmental footprint of supply chain activities. Key strategies include reducing greenhouse gas emissions, optimizing resource utilization, advancing waste reduction, and implementing renewable energy solutions.

- Ethical Practices in the Supply Chain: This pillar focuses on ensuring that all stages of the supply chain adhere to high ethical standards. It encompasses maintaining fair labor practices, ensuring workplace safety, upholding human rights, enforcing transparent business practices, and engaging in responsible sourcing.

- Economic Sustainability: While prioritizing environmental and social aspects, sustainable SCM also ensures economic feasibility. This includes creating cost-effective, sustainable models that foster long-term growth and stability.

Role of Lean Six Sigma in Advancing Sustainable SCM

LSS methodologies are instrumental in integrating sustainability into SCM:

- Lean Approaches for Waste Minimization: Lean principles are employed to systematically reduce waste in supply chain processes, which not only improves efficiency but also lessens environmental impact.

- Optimizing Processes with Six Sigma: The Six Sigma approach is utilized to enhance process efficiency, ensuring that resources are optimally utilized, thereby supporting both environmental and economic sustainability.

- Sustainable Supplier Management: LSS methodologies aid in the selection and evaluation of suppliers based on their commitment to sustainable practices, thereby extending ethical and environmental standards across the supply chain.

- Promoting Continuous Sustainable Improvement: The LSS framework of continuous assessment and refinement ensures that sustainability efforts are not static but evolve to meet new environmental challenges and leverage emerging technologies.

Challenges and Strategies in Implementing Sustainable SCM

Implementing sustainable SCM practices, particularly through LSS, involves navigating various challenges:

- Balancing Initial Costs with Long-Term Gains: Transitioning to sustainable practices often incurs initial costs, but these must be viewed as investments in long-term sustainability.
- Addressing Resistance to Change: Resistance from stakeholders, both within and outside the organization, can impede sustainable SCM initiatives. Effective communication, education, and stakeholder engagement are vital in overcoming this barrier.
- Measuring and Quantifying Sustainability: Assessing the impact of sustainability initiatives, especially in ethical and indirect environmental aspects, requires robust and comprehensive metrics and measurement systems.

Conclusion: The Imperative of Sustainable SCM

In the modern business landscape, sustainability in SCM is not just an option but a necessity. Integrating ethical and environmental considerations into SCM, guided by Lean Six Sigma principles, offers a pathway for supply chains to become more responsible and sustainable. This approach ensures that organizations not only achieve operational efficiency and cost-effectiveness but also contribute positively to societal and environmental welfare. This chapter highlights the critical role of sustainability in SCM, underscoring its importance in meeting present needs without compromising future resources and ethical standards.

Chapter 21: Practical Insights: Case Studies in LSS-Driven SCM

Introduction: Unveiling the Practical Impact of Lean Six Sigma in SCM

In the complex world of Supply Chain Management (SCM), Lean Six Sigma (LSS) emerges as a transformative methodology, crucial for enhancing efficiency, reducing costs, and improving customer satisfaction. This chapter offers a comprehensive exploration of LSS's real-world applications across various industries, providing a deeper understanding of its practical challenges, benefits, and strategic implications in SCM.

Diverse Industry Perspectives: Case Studies of LSS in SCM

LSS's versatility is exemplified in its application across multiple sectors, each presenting unique challenges and yielding significant gains:

1. Toyota's Lean Mastery in the Automotive Industry

   - Implementation Strategy: Toyota's integration of the Toyota Production System (TPS) exemplifies Lean's application in optimizing supply chain operations.
   - Key Tactics: Emphasizing Just-In-Time (JIT) inventory management and continuous improvement (Kaizen) principles.
   - Outcomes and Benefits: This approach achieved a drastic reduction in waste and lead times, leading to enhanced operational efficiency and substantial cost savings.
   - Broader Implications: Toyota's success illustrates how Lean principles can revolutionize industry standards and influence global supply chain practices.

2. Amazon's Six Sigma Excellence in Retail

   - Implementation Approach: Amazon employed Six Sigma methodologies to refine its vast, intricate supply chain.
   - Focus Areas: Concentrating on error minimization, process optimization, and customer satisfaction enhancement.
   - Results Achieved: Streamlining of the supply chain, ensuring timely deliveries, and reduction in operational costs.
   - Industry Impact: Amazon's case underscores the importance of precision and customer-centricity in SCM for retail giants.

3. Stanford Health Care's LSS Transformation in Healthcare
   - Implementation Details: The adoption of LSS for improving supply chain processes, particularly in order processing and inventory management.
   - Methodology: Leveraging process mapping and root cause analysis to identify and address inefficiencies.
   - Key Outcomes: Enhanced efficiency in the supply chain, reduced stockouts, and notable cost savings.
   - Sector-specific Insights: This case study highlights the critical role of LSS in addressing the unique challenges of healthcare supply chains.

4. Samsung's SCM Innovations in Electronics
   - LSS Integration: Applying LSS for supply chain enhancements focused on quality and inventory management.
   - DMAIC Application: Utilization of Define, Measure, Analyze, Improve, Control (DMAIC) for continuous process improvement.
   - Achievements: Significant improvements in product quality, supplier performance, and operational efficiency.
   - Industry Lessons: The case exemplifies the role of LSS in maintaining competitiveness in the fast-paced electronics sector.

Challenges and Learnings from LSS Implementations

These case studies collectively reveal essential challenges and lessons:

- Customization and Flexibility: Tailoring LSS principles to suit distinct organizational needs, scales, and complexities is critical for success.
- Navigating Cultural Shifts: Effective LSS integration often requires substantial cultural and operational shifts within organizations. Success hinges on robust change management and stakeholder engagement strategies.
- Sustaining Continuous Improvement: The ongoing nature of LSS necessitates a long-term commitment to continuous improvement, adapting to market changes and evolving business environments.

Conclusion: Broadening the Scope of LSS in SCM

The application of Lean Six Sigma across these diverse industries demonstrates its adaptability and efficacy in optimizing supply chains. These real-world cases underscore the need for strategic customization, stakeholder engagement, and a commitment to perpetual improvement. They serve as both a source of inspiration and a practical blueprint for organizations looking to harness LSS for SCM optimization. This chapter solidifies LSS's role as a fundamental tool for achieving sustainable, efficient, and customer-oriented supply chain transformations in various business landscapes.

Chapter 22: SCM's Future: Embracing Digital Trends and LSS Adaptation

Introduction: Charting the Digital Evolution in SCM

The landscape of Supply Chain Management (SCM) is experiencing a seismic shift due to the integration of digital technologies, reshaping traditional practices and strategies. This transformation, complemented by the adaptation of Lean Six Sigma (LSS) methodologies to the digital context, is setting the stage for innovative and efficient SCM models. This chapter delves into the dynamic interplay between emerging digital trends and LSS adaptations, examining their profound impact on the future of SCM.

Disruptive Digital Technologies Transforming SCM

Several key digital innovations are redefining SCM processes:

- Advanced Capabilities of AI and ML: These technologies are revolutionizing SCM with predictive analytics for precise demand forecasting, inventory management optimization, and creating personalized customer experiences.
- IoT Enhancements in Real-Time Monitoring: IoT technology enables unprecedented real-time tracking, providing crucial data on goods, environmental conditions, and equipment health. This facilitates proactive maintenance, enhancing SCM reliability and reducing downtime.
- Blockchain for Transparency and Security: Blockchain's potential in SCM lies in its ability to create transparent, immutable records, ideal for tracking product origins, verifying ethical sourcing practices, and preventing fraud.
- Robotic Automation and Efficiency: The integration of robotics in warehouses and the exploration of drones for delivery services are pivotal in automating tasks, elevating operational efficiency, and reducing manual errors.
- VR and AR in Operational Planning and Execution: VR's application in warehouse design and supply chain disruption planning, alongside AR's role in enhancing operational tasks like order picking, exemplifies how these technologies are optimizing SCM environments.

LSS Adaptations in the Digital SCM Era

Adapting LSS principles to digital trends involves strategic innovations:

- Data-Driven Precision in LSS: The abundance of data from digital tools enriches the Measure and Analyze phases of LSS, leading to refined insights and more impactful decision-making.
- Process Optimization Prior to Automation: LSS principles are critical in ensuring processes are streamlined before automation, thereby amplifying efficiency rather than inefficiencies.
- Leveraging Digital Twins for LSS Experimentation: The use of digital twins in LSS facilitates efficient process change simulations, improving the efficiency of Design of Experiments and pilot testing.

- Broadening VoC Through Digital Channels: The expansion of VoC in the Define phase of LSS is enhanced by the wealth of customer feedback available through digital platforms, ensuring a customer-centric approach in SCM processes.

Navigating Challenges and Seizing Opportunities in Digital SCM

The digital transformation of SCM presents unique challenges and opportunities:

- Addressing the Digital-LSS Skill Gap: The increasing reliance on digital tools in SCM creates a demand for professionals proficient in both digital technologies and LSS methodologies.
- Data Security and Privacy Prioritization: The proliferation of digital data necessitates stringent security measures and adherence to privacy standards.
- Keeping Pace with Technological Advancements: Continuous adaptation of LSS principles is required to stay aligned with the rapid evolution of digital tools in SCM.

Conclusion: Forging a New Path in SCM

The synergy between digital innovations and LSS methodologies is forging a new path in SCM. This convergence offers unprecedented opportunities for enhancing efficiency, agility, and customer responsiveness. Organizations that successfully integrate these advancements are setting new benchmarks in SCM, positioning themselves for competitive advantage and sustainable growth. This chapter emphasizes the critical role of embracing digital trends and adapting LSS methodologies to stay at the forefront of SCM evolution.

Chapter 23: Conclusion: The Path to Supply Chain Excellence with LSS

Introduction: Harnessing LSS for Advanced SCM

In the contemporary landscape of Supply Chain Management (SCM), Lean Six Sigma (LSS) has emerged as a vital methodology for achieving excellence. This chapter encapsulates the journey through LSS principles, illustrating their transformative impact on SCM. It delves into how LSS methodologies act as catalysts for operational efficiency, quality enhancement, and strategic SCM innovation.

Core Principles of LSS in Transforming SCM

LSS integrates critical principles that drive significant improvements in SCM:

- Streamlining Operations with Lean: Lean principles are crucial in eliminating waste across SCM processes, leading to streamlined operations, efficient resource utilization, and substantial cost savings.
- Quality Assurance via Six Sigma: Six Sigma's focus on minimizing errors and variability ensures high-quality outcomes in SCM activities, directly influencing customer satisfaction and reliability.
- Strategic Decision-Making Through Data Analysis: LSS emphasizes data-driven decision-making, enhancing accuracy in forecasting, risk management, and strategic planning within SCM.

Expansive Application of LSS Across SCM Activities

LSS extends its influence across various segments of SCM:

- Efficient Inventory Management: LSS guides effective inventory control strategies, balancing just-in-time stock levels and reducing overstock and shortages.
- Enhanced Supplier Relationships and Collaboration: Applying LSS in supplier management fosters improved quality control, efficiency, and mutual benefits in supplier partnerships.
- Logistics and Distribution Optimization: LSS methodologies contribute to more efficient logistics, including optimized routing, cost-effective transportation, and enhanced delivery capabilities.
- Promotion of Sustainable SCM Practices: Aligning LSS with sustainability goals aids in developing SCM practices that are environmentally responsible and ethically sound.

Overcoming Challenges and Fostering a Culture of Change

Implementing LSS in SCM involves navigating numerous challenges:

- Navigating Organizational Change: The adoption of LSS necessitates a shift in organizational culture, emphasizing the need for effective leadership, change management, and continuous training.
- Technological Integration and Advancements: As SCM adopts advanced digital tools, LSS must evolve to incorporate these technologies, leveraging data analytics for enhanced process improvement.

- Global SCM Dynamics: Adapting LSS to the complexities of global supply chains requires an understanding of diverse market conditions, cultural factors, and geopolitical influences.

The Continuous Journey of Improvement and Adaptation

LSS in SCM is an ongoing process, characterized by continuous improvement and adaptation:

- Commitment to Kaizen: Embracing the principle of continuous improvement is key to maintaining long-term efficiency and effectiveness in SCM operations.
- Adaptation to Emerging SCM Trends: LSS methodologies must be dynamic, evolving in response to new SCM challenges, market trends, and technological advancements.
- Encouraging Innovation within LSS Framework: Innovation within the LSS framework can lead to groundbreaking improvements, fostering a culture of experimentation and forward-thinking in SCM.

Conclusion: Charting a Future of Excellence with LSS in SCM

Lean Six Sigma offers a comprehensive, structured approach to mastering SCM. Its emphasis on efficiency, quality, and strategic improvement positions it as an essential tool for building robust, agile, and customer-focused supply chains. As SCM continues to evolve, LSS stands as a guiding methodology, providing the strategies and tools necessary for navigating the complexities of modern supply chains. This chapter concludes by reaffirming the essential role of LSS in driving SCM towards a future of operational excellence, sustainability, and competitive success in the global business arena.

Appendix A: Essential SCM and LSS Terminology

This appendix serves as a comprehensive glossary, elucidating key terms and concepts in Supply Chain Management (SCM) and Lean Six Sigma (LSS) that are crucial for understanding the methodologies, strategies, and practices discussed in this book.

- Lean: A systematic approach to minimizing waste without sacrificing productivity.
- Six Sigma: A method that focuses on process improvement and variation reduction.
- DMAIC (Define, Measure, Analyze, Improve, Control): A data-driven quality strategy used to improve processes.
- Kaizen (Continuous Improvement): The practice of making small, incremental changes routinely to improve efficiency and quality.
- Just-In-Time (JIT): An inventory strategy companies employ to increase efficiency and decrease waste by receiving goods only as they are needed.
- Value Stream Mapping: A lean-management method for analyzing the current state and designing a future state for the series of events that take a product or service from its beginning through to the customer.
- Kanban: An inventory-control system used in just-in-time manufacturing.
- Supply Chain Optimization: The application of processes and tools to ensure the optimal operation of a manufacturing and distribution supply chain.
- Logistics: The detailed coordination of a complex operation involving many people, facilities, or supplies.
- 5S (Sort, Set in order, Shine, Standardize, Sustain): A workplace organization method that uses a list of five Japanese words: seiri, seiton, seiso, seiketsu, and shitsuke.
- Muda (Waste): Activities that don't add value and are considered waste.
- Total Quality Management (TQM): A management approach to long-term success through customer satisfaction.
- Bottleneck Analysis: The process of identifying the points in a process where workloads build up or slow down.
- Inventory Turnover: A ratio showing how many times a company has sold and replaced inventory during a given period.
- Cycle Time: The total time from the beginning to the end of your process, as defined by you and your customer.
- Root Cause Analysis: A method of problem-solving used for identifying the root causes of faults or problems.
- SCOR Model (Supply Chain Operations Reference model): A management tool used to address, improve, and communicate supply chain management decisions within a company.

Appendix B: Comprehensive Models in Supply Chain Management

This appendix outlines various models and frameworks in SCM, providing an in-depth look at the methodologies that have shaped modern supply chain management.

- Push and Pull Strategy: This model is based on consumer demand - in 'push' strategy, inventory is pushed onto the market, whereas in 'pull', production is based on consumer demand.
- SCOR Model (Supply Chain Operations Reference model): This model is a comprehensive model of the core management processes and metrics in supply chain management.
- Agile Supply Chain: This model focuses on responsiveness and adaptability, with an emphasis on customer satisfaction and the ability to adapt to changes in the market quickly.
- Lean Supply Chain: Similar to Lean manufacturing, this model focuses on minimizing waste within the supply chain, optimizing processes, and delivering value to the customer.
- Green Supply Chain Management: This model focuses on environmental aspects and sustainability in the supply chain, seeking to minimize the ecological footprint of products and processes.
- Global Supply Chain Model: This model addresses the complexities of managing supply chains in a global context, dealing with multinational logistics, cross-cultural communication, and various international regulations.
- Demand-Driven Supply Chain (DDSC): This approach is focused on building supply chains that are driven by precise customer demands rather than mere market predictions.
- Resilient Supply Chain Model: This model prioritizes the ability of a supply chain to anticipate, adapt to, and rapidly recover from disruptions, whether internal or external.

Understanding these terms, concepts, and models is essential for grasping the complexities of SCM and LSS, providing a solid foundation for exploring the more advanced strategies and applications discussed in the book.

Appendix C: Core Lean Six Sigma Tools and Techniques

This comprehensive appendix delves into the essential tools and techniques at the heart of Lean Six Sigma (LSS), offering a detailed exploration of their functions, applications, and relevance in optimizing Supply Chain Management (SCM).

- Value Stream Mapping (VSM): An essential tool for visualizing and analyzing the steps involved in taking a product from start to finish, highlighting areas of waste and opportunities for streamlining processes.
- 5 Whys Technique: A root cause analysis tool that involves asking "Why" repeatedly until the fundamental cause of a problem is identified, promoting deeper understanding and more effective solutions.
- DMAIC Framework: Standing for Define, Measure, Analyze, Improve, and Control, this structured methodology guides process improvement initiatives through a rigorous data-driven approach.
- Pareto Analysis (80/20 Rule): This principle is used to identify the few critical factors that contribute to the majority of a problem's impact, enabling focused and effective problem-solving efforts.
- Fishbone Diagram (Ishikawa/Cause and Effect): A visual tool used for categorizing potential causes of problems to identify root causes, fostering comprehensive analysis of issues.
- Kanban System: A scheduling system that enhances just-in-time (JIT) production, Kanban helps in managing workflow and inventory at each stage of the supply chain.
- Control Charts: These statistical tools are used to analyze process stability over time and identify variations that signify underlying problems in SCM processes.
- FMEA (Failure Modes and Effects Analysis): A systematic approach for anticipating potential failures in processes or products and implementing strategies to mitigate risk.
- Gemba Walks: Involves going to the actual place where work is done (the 'gemba') to observe and understand the real-world workings of processes, identifying areas for improvement.
- SIPOC Diagrams: This high-level view of processes, outlining Suppliers, Inputs, Process, Outputs, and Customers, provides a macro perspective on how processes operate and interact.
- Process Mapping: Creating detailed workflow diagrams that illustrate the sequence of steps in a process, aiding in the identification of inefficiencies and opportunities for improvement.
- Advanced Six Sigma Tools: Including statistical tools used for in-depth process analysis, such as hypothesis testing, regression analysis, and design of experiments, typically employed by Green Belts and Black Belts.

Appendix D: Compliance and Standards in SCM

This appendix offers an in-depth look at the compliance and standards integral to SCM, emphasizing their role in ensuring ethical, efficient, and sustainable supply chain practices.

- ISO Standards: These international standards, including ISO 9001 and ISO 14001, provide guidelines for quality and environmental management in SCM.
- Legal Compliance: Compliance with local and international laws is crucial, encompassing labor laws, environmental regulations, trade agreements, and customs laws.
- Ethical Sourcing and Labor Standards: Adherence to ethical sourcing standards is vital, ensuring that products are made respecting human rights and labor laws.
- Sustainability Standards: Standards and frameworks such as the Carbon Disclosure Project and the Dow Jones Sustainability Indices guide sustainable practices in SCM.
- C-TPAT Compliance: This voluntary program aims to improve the security of private companies' supply chains against terrorism threats.
- Blockchain for Transparency: The use of blockchain in SCM enhances transparency and traceability, ensuring adherence to standards and reducing fraud.
- Data Protection and Privacy: Compliance with data protection regulations like GDPR is essential in managing sensitive customer and vendor data.
- Quality Audits and Certifications: Regular audits and certifications like Six Sigma certifications validate the efficiency and quality of SCM processes.

Understanding and utilizing these LSS tools and adhering to SCM standards and compliance regulations are crucial for professionals aiming to optimize supply chains efficiently, responsibly, and sustainably.

Appendix E: Best Practices and Pitfalls in SCM LSS Implementation

This appendix presents an exhaustive discussion of the key practices and common pitfalls in the implementation of Lean Six Sigma (LSS) within Supply Chain Management (SCM), offering a detailed roadmap for effective integration and optimization.

Best Practices in SCM LSS Implementation
- Integrating LSS with Organizational Strategy: Aligning LSS projects with the company's strategic vision ensures SCM improvements contribute meaningfully to business goals and objectives.
- Comprehensive Stakeholder Engagement: Involving all stakeholders, including top management, SCM teams, suppliers, and customers in the LSS initiative fosters a collaborative environment crucial for successful implementation.
- Focused Training and Skill Development: Implementing a robust training program to equip SCM personnel with LSS tools and methodologies enhances the team's capability to drive improvements effectively.
- Adopting a Data-Driven Methodology: Utilizing data analytics and statistical tools in decision-making processes ensures SCM improvements are factual and objective.
- Cultivating a Continuous Improvement Mindset: Encouraging a culture that values ongoing refinement and optimization within the SCM team is key to sustaining long-term improvements.
- Effective Pilot Testing: Implementing pilot projects prior to full-scale rollouts helps identify potential issues and fine-tune processes, mitigating risks of large-scale failures.

Common Pitfalls in SCM LSS Implementation
- Lack of Leadership Commitment: Inadequate support and involvement from senior leadership can significantly diminish the impact and sustainability of LSS initiatives in SCM.
- Organizational Resistance to Change: Overcoming resistance, often stemming from a lack of understanding or fear of the unknown, is crucial for the successful adoption of LSS methodologies.
- Resource Allocation Challenges: Insufficient allocation of resources, including personnel, time, and budget, can limit the scope and effectiveness of LSS projects.
- Neglecting Customer Insights: Failure to incorporate customer feedback and preferences can lead to SCM improvements that are misaligned with market needs.
- Complex Solution Implementation: Introducing overly complicated LSS solutions can lead to confusion, reduced efficiency, and process bottlenecks.

Appendix F: Sample Templates for SCM and Lean Six Sigma

This appendix provides a collection of essential templates and tools, serving as practical aids in applying LSS within SCM.

- SIPOC Diagram Template: Outlines a comprehensive view of SCM processes, helping teams visualize and understand the workflow from beginning to end.
- Value Stream Mapping Template: Assists in analyzing the flow of materials and information in SCM processes, identifying inefficiencies and opportunities for improvement.
- Fishbone Diagram Template: A structured tool for brainstorming potential causes of SCM problems and pinpointing areas for improvement.
- DMAIC Project Charter Template: A foundational document for LSS projects in SCM, detailing project scope, objectives, timelines, and team roles.
- 5 Whys Analysis Template: A straightforward approach for conducting root cause analysis in SCM, promoting deeper problem-solving.
- Control Chart Template: Aids in monitoring and assessing the stability of SCM processes over time, identifying variations and trends.
- FMEA Template: Helps in proactively identifying potential failure modes in SCM processes and products and developing strategies to mitigate risks.
- Kanban Board Template: Visualizes task management and workflow in SCM operations, optimizing efficiency and resource allocation.
- Gemba Walk Checklist: Provides guidelines for conducting effective Gemba Walks within SCM environments, focusing on operational insights and improvement opportunities.

Utilizing these best practices and templates can significantly enhance the effectiveness and efficiency of LSS implementation in SCM, leading to streamlined processes, reduced costs, and improved organizational performance.

Appendix G: Global Best Practices in SCM

This appendix offers an exhaustive examination of best practices in Supply Chain Management (SCM) observed globally, derived from a spectrum of industries and market environments. These practices represent the pinnacle of SCM effectiveness and efficiency, providing a template for excellence in various contexts.

Key Global SCM Best Practices

- Agility and Flexibility in Supply Chains: Emphasizing the need for adaptable and responsive supply chain structures that can swiftly adjust to market shifts and disruptions.

- Comprehensive Risk Management: Implementing robust strategies for risk assessment and mitigation, crucial for managing the complexities and uncertainties inherent in global supply chains.

- Sustainability and Ethical Operations: Prioritizing environmental stewardship and ethical practices throughout the supply chain, responding to increasing consumer and regulatory demands for corporate responsibility.

- Data-Driven Strategic Decision-Making: Employing advanced analytics and big data to extract actionable insights, leading to informed decisions that optimize supply chain operations.

- Building Collaborative Supplier Networks: Fostering strong, strategic partnerships with suppliers to ensure quality, reliability, and continuous innovation within the supply chain.

- Investment in Workforce Capability: Concentrating on enhancing the skills and knowledge of SCM professionals to keep pace with evolving industry practices and technological advancements.

- Customer-Centric Supply Chain Models: Aligning supply chain processes closely with customer needs and feedback to enhance service quality and overall satisfaction.

- Adherence to International SCM Standards: Ensuring compliance with global standards and regulations to maintain quality, safety, and legality in international supply chain operations.

Appendix H: Amalgamation of Disruptive Technologies, SCM, and LSS

This appendix explores how the convergence of disruptive technologies with SCM and Lean Six Sigma (LSS) is revolutionizing supply chain strategies and operations, offering insights into future trends and implementation methodologies.

Integrating Cutting-Edge Technologies in SCM and LSS

- AI and Machine Learning for Enhanced SCM: Utilizing AI and ML for advanced predictive analytics and demand forecasting, integrating these insights with LSS for process improvement and optimization.
- IoT for Real-Time SCM Monitoring: Implementing IoT devices to enable real-time tracking and monitoring, enhancing decision-making and operational efficiency in line with LSS principles.
- Blockchain for Secure, Transparent SCM: Applying blockchain technology to create secure, transparent supply chain transactions, thus enhancing traceability and reducing potential fraud.
- Robotics and Automation in Line with Lean Principles: Incorporating robotics and automation in logistics and warehousing to improve efficiency and accuracy, in alignment with Lean methodologies.
- Use of AR and VR for SCM Optimization: Leveraging AR and VR for immersive training and simulation of supply chain scenarios, aiding in identifying potential improvements and efficiencies.
- Big Data Analytics in Strategic SCM Decision-Making: Integrating big data analytics to provide comprehensive insights for strategic SCM decisions, complementing the data-driven nature of LSS.
- Digital Twins for Advanced Process Simulation: Employing digital twin technology to model and simulate SCM processes for effective improvement and optimization, in accordance with LSS methodologies.

Challenges and Opportunities in Technological Integration

The merger of disruptive technologies with SCM and LSS poses challenges but also opens up vast opportunities:

- Addressing the Skills Gap: Ensuring that SCM professionals are adept in both advanced technologies and LSS methodologies for effective implementation.
- Maintaining Data Security and Regulatory Compliance: Managing the complexities of data security and staying compliant with evolving regulations in the digital age.
- Embracing Continuous Adaptation and Innovation: Keeping up with rapid technological advancements to continuously enhance and innovate SCM processes.

These appendices collectively provide a detailed guide to the best practices and technological integrations shaping modern SCM, offering valuable insights for professionals seeking to navigate and excel in the dynamic world of global supply chain management.

Appendix I: Integrating Disruptive Technologies with SCM and Lean Six Sigma

This comprehensive appendix delves into the integration of disruptive technologies with Supply Chain Management (SCM) and Lean Six Sigma (LSS), offering a detailed analysis of how this convergence can drive transformative improvements in SCM processes.

Detailed Overview of Disruptive Technologies in SCM and LSS

1. Artificial Intelligence (AI) and Machine Learning (ML):

   - Function: AI and ML provide predictive insights into consumer behavior, supply needs, and market trends. They enable advanced data processing for demand forecasting and inventory optimization.
   - Integration with LSS: These technologies can enhance the Analyze phase in DMAIC by providing deeper data insights, thereby leading to more informed process improvements.

2. Internet of Things (IoT):

   - Function: IoT facilitates real-time tracking of products, machinery performance, and environmental conditions in warehouses, offering data critical for process monitoring and decision-making.
   - Integration with LSS: IoT data can be used in the Control phase of LSS to continuously monitor process variations and implement real-time corrective actions.

3. Blockchain Technology:

   - Function: Blockchain introduces enhanced transparency and security in SCM operations, particularly in tracking product origins and ensuring compliance with ethical sourcing standards.
   - Integration with LSS: Blockchain's data integrity is crucial for reliable process analysis and maintaining quality standards in SCM.

4. Robotics and Automation:

   - Function: Robotics automate repetitive tasks in warehouses and production lines, increasing efficiency and reducing human error.
   - Integration with LSS: Automation aligns with Lean's waste reduction philosophy and can be used to optimize the efficiency of processes identified in the Improve phase.

5. Augmented Reality (AR) and Virtual Reality (VR):

   - Function: AR and VR are used for training, visualizing complex supply chain networks, and simulating different SCM scenarios for planning.

- Integration with LSS: These technologies can play a role in training staff on LSS principles and simulating the impact of proposed process changes.

6. Big Data Analytics:
- Function: Big data analytics involves examining large sets of data to uncover hidden patterns and unknown correlations.
- Integration with LSS: Big data can inform the Measure phase of LSS by providing extensive insights into process performance.

Strategies for Successful Integration
- Business Goal Alignment: Ensuring that the introduction of new technologies is in line with the strategic objectives of the organization and complements the LSS initiatives.
- Comprehensive Training Programs: Developing training modules for staff to skillfully integrate technology with LSS methodologies.
- Pilot Programs and Gradual Implementation: Initiating small-scale pilot programs to evaluate the effectiveness of technology integration with LSS before wider deployment.
- Emphasis on Data Security and Regulatory Compliance: Implementing robust security measures to protect data integrity and ensure compliance with industry regulations.
- Continuous Monitoring and Evaluation: Establishing mechanisms for ongoing assessment and refinement of the technology-LSS integration.
- Effective Change Management: Employing change management strategies to ease the transition to new technologies and processes.

Challenges and Key Considerations
- Assessing Technological Compatibility: Evaluating how new technologies can be seamlessly integrated with existing SCM systems and LSS practices.
- Conducting Cost-Benefit Analysis: Thoroughly analyzing the financial implications and potential ROI of integrating new technologies.
- Keeping Up with Technological Evolution: Staying informed about emerging technologies and their potential applications in SCM and LSS.

The strategic integration of disruptive technologies with SCM and LSS represents a significant opportunity for modern businesses to enhance their supply chain efficiency, quality, and responsiveness. This appendix not only outlines the potential of such integration but also provides a roadmap for effective implementation, ensuring organizations can fully leverage these technologies to gain a competitive edge in their SCM operations.

www.ingramcontent.com/pod-product-compliance
Ingram Content Group UK Ltd.
Pitfield, Milton Keynes, MK11 3LW, UK
UKHW060217240426
12048UKWH00030BB/1703